T0329453

THE BOOK OF WAR

THE BOOK OF WAR

FROM THE SERIES
TALES OF THE DRAGON

LONG TANG

Algora Publishing
New York

Library of Congress Cataloging-in-Publication Data —

Names: Tang, Long, author.
Title: The book of war / Long Tang.
Description: New York: Algora Publishing, [2017] | Series: Tales of the
  dragon | Includes bibliographical references and index.
Identifiers: LCCN 2017017491 (print) | LCCN 2017017785 (ebook) | ISBN
  9781628942934 (pdf) | ISBN 9781628942910 (soft cover: alk. paper) | ISBN
  9781628942927 (hard cover: alk. paper)
Subjects: LCSH: China—History, Military—To 221 B.C. | China—History—To
  221 B.C.—Biography.
Classification: LCC DS741.72 (ebook) | LCC DS741.72 .L65 2018 (print) | DDC
  355.00931/09014—dc23
LC record available at https://lccn.loc.gov/2017017491

Printed in the United States

With sincere appreciation to:

      Jie Li, Kimberly Fu-hsing Tang and Shirley Branch
         for the cover design
      John Wang for the cover calligraphy
      Dana Lynne Tang for spiritual support
      Arlington Writers Group for critical critique and support

Other books by Long TANG:

Tales of the Dragon: The Book of Lore
Pets Only (co-authored with Shadow Tang)

Table of Contents

PREFACE   1

CHAPTER 1. MILITARY ORGANIZATION OF ANCIENT CHINA   3
   War chariots   5
   Command and Control   7

CHAPTER 2. ANCIENT CHINESE WEAPONS AND EQUIPMENT   11
   Equipment   11
      Traction Trebuchet   11
      The Bed Crossbow   13
      The Nest Cart   14
      The Cloud Ladder   15
      Pontoon Bridge   15

   Defensive Equipment   16
      Flying Hook, Wolf Fang Smasher   16
      The Witches' Thunder   16
      The Door Jammer   17

   Gun Powder Weapons   17
   Personal Weapons   19
   Personal Protective Equipment   21

CHAPTER 3. STRATEGIC CULTURAL THINKING   23

CHAPTER 4. THE CULTURAL PARADIGM   29

CHAPTER 5. SIX ARTS, THE MAKING OF A KNIGHT   33

CHAPTER 6. SAN YANG, THE IRON CHANCELLOR, ARCHITECT OF
   IMPERIAL CHINA   39

CHAPTER 7. BAI CHI, THE MOST SUCCESSFUL GENERAL IN CHINESE
   HISTORY   47
   Three of Bai Chi's signature campaigns   48

I. The Battle of Yi Jue (293 BC).   48
II. The Battles of Yan and Ying (279 BC)   51
III. The Battle of Chang-Ping (260 BC)   52

CHAPTER 8. GAN LUO, THE DIPLOMATIC GENIUS   65

CHAPTER 9. KONG MING, THE CHINESE LEONARDO DA VINCI   67

CHAPTER 10. WU QI, THE FLAWED PERFECT GENERAL   71
The Elite Warrior Corps (Wu Ju Zhi)   75
Wu Qi Returns to the Court   76
Wu Qi Implements His Civil Ideas   78

CHAPTER 11. SUN BIN AND 'MAKE THEM RIDE TO THE SOUND OF THE BATTLE'   81

CHAPTER 12. ZHAO SER AND THE GREAT FAKE   85
Strategies of Zhao Ser   85

CHAPTER 13. YU XU AND DECEPTION, DECEPTION AND MORE DECEPTION   89

CHAPTER 14. XIANG YU AND THE STRATEGY OF SMASHED STOVES AND SUNKEN SHIPS   91

CHAPTER 15. THE PEASANT AND THE WARRIOR: THE FOUNDING OF THE IMPERIAL HAN EMPIRE   95

CHAPTER 16. THE BARE HEAD BRIGADE, BERSERKER TROOPS OF ANCIENT CHINA   103

CHAPTER 17. PSYCHOLOGICAL WARFARE, 285 BC   109

CHAPTER 18. THE BATTLE OF THE RED CLIFF, THE SALAMIS OF ANCIENT CHINA   117

CHAPTER 19. THE BATTLE OF BO-JU, SUN TZU'S SIGNATURE CAMPAIGN   121

CHAPTER 20. THE BATTLE OF ZUI-LI, THE BATTLE THAT SUN TZU LOST   125

CHAPTER 21. THE PATH OF VENGEANCE   127

CHAPTER 22. BATTLE OF JIN-YANG, THE END OF THE SPRING AND AUTUMN ERA   131

CHAPTER 23. ZHENG HE, THE ADMIRAL   135

CHAPTER 24. JING KE, THE DEATH WARRIOR   139

CHAPTER 25. MO DAO, THE FORERUNNER OF THE SAMURAI SWORD   159

CHAPTER 26. CHINESE CROSSBOWS   165

BIBLIOGRAPHY   173

INDEX   175

PREFACE

The Art of War by Sun Tzu gives us Chinese theories on warfare. *Tales of the Dragon — The Book of War* chronicles the military organization, equipment, key personalities, and major campaigns that produced China.

This book focuses predominantly on ancient Chinese military history from 500 BC to 200 BC. Military accomplishments and developments of that era left an indelible legacy in the field of warfare for ensuing generations to study and learn.

According to the Chinese Military History Society at the Department of History, Kansas State University, "No comprehensive survey of Chinese military history is yet available in English." *Tales of the Dragon — The Book of War* addresses that shortfall.

* * *

The Imperial Chinese Empire was the product of over five hundred years of continuous warfare that took place in the latter part of the Zhou Dynasty (1122–256 BC). Initially, the King of Zhou ruled as the leader of an alliance with over 1,800 subordinate feudal states. The erosion of central authority led to power struggles, assimilations and conquest. By the time of the Spring and Autumn Era (770–476 BC) and the ensuing Warring States Era (476–221 BC), near the end of the Zhou Dynasty, the 1,800 feudal states had dwindled to a mere score.

Seven powerful lords dominated central China. The Ch'in and the Chu, the strongest of those seven, were able to field million men armies each, while the other five could individually marshal 300,000–400,000 soldiers into one battle. At the time, taking a 100,000 heads in one single campaign was not uncommon. Such major military undertakings created standardized military organizations, equipment, and weaponry; more significantly they produced commanders that were at least equal, if not superior, to Alexander, Caesar and Napoleon in terms of skills and achievements.

CHAPTER 1. MILITARY ORGANIZATION OF ANCIENT CHINA

The early Chinese military system evolved with the consolidation of small tribal villages into feudal states. Initially (circa 2100 BC), rulers filled their military ranks with feudal levies. In the ensuing eras, the increasingly large scale of warfare brought a higher demand for military manpower and resulted in the institution of conscription. But it was a haphazard arrangement until 358 BC, when the Ch'in kingdom established a regimented universal draft infrastructure, in which all males 17 to 60 had to register with the magistrate. Every registrant owed the realm two months of labor service each year. Starting at age 23, the men became eligible for the military draft, serving one year in outlying provinces, and one year at the national capital of Xian-Yang or the frontier posts; plus wartime levies.

In 221 BC, the Ch'in kingdom unified China and its conscription system carried over into the following imperial empires. However, the military draft was modified by ensuing dynasties according to the needs of the realm. Basically, the armed forces consisted of central, provincial and frontier units. The emperor sent central government units to meet military emergencies. Provincial and frontier units supported the central government units as needed. During peacetime, provincial units were reduced to save money and minimize their threats to the central government. In times of war, the central government recruited volunteers to augment shortfalls in levies.

The Han Dynasty (206 BC–AD 220) required a strong military to counter the nomadic threat. It used three strategies to fight the barbarian. First, it encouraged people on the frontiers to raise horses for the cavalry in exchange for reduced taxes; second, friendly and defeated nomadic tribes were recruited to fight the belligerent nomads, not unlike the Roman handling of the Gauls; third, convicts, prisoners and people who offended the emperor were sent to serve in frontier posts. At times, entire families, clans or tribes were exiled to settle in the border regions.

The maritime forces of early China operated primarily in rivers and lakes in south and central China, where waterways dominated the terrain. The Chinese did not develop a large ocean-going navy until the 14th century, and that effort was ended after the death of Admiral Zheng He in AD 1433.

* * *

Excavations of Shang Dynasty tombs (1523–1046 BC) have revealed that the early Chinese used *Wu* (伍), a unit of five, as the basic element of a military formation. The word *Wu* also came to represent things related to military organizations. A "*Wu*" was equivalent to a fire team in the modern infantry. Each *Wu* had a leader called the Tun Zhang. Five *Wu*'s constituted a *Liang* (兩) of 25 men, commanded by a Liang Shima. A *Liang* could be equated to a modern-day platoon. Four *Liang*'s (platoons) formed a *Zu* (卒) of 100 men, led by a *Zu* leader. The *Zu* would be equivalent to a company or troop in the modern military force. Five *Zu*'s made a *Lu* (旅) of 500 men, about the size of a battalion. Five *Lu*'s constituted a *Shi* (師) of 2,500 men. Five Shi's became a 12,500 men *Jun* (军), which was commanded by a general. This basic military configuration remained with minor variations until the 20th century.

Three *Jun*'s were the standard size of a standing army maintained by kingdoms of the Warring States Era, but larger kingdoms had a standing army of as many as six *Jun*'s.

www.bigstock.com · 2100052

2. Chinese War Chariot (big.stock.com)

4

In the post-imperial era, China adopted a Western military organizational structure. A platoon was called a *Pai* (排); a company became a *Lian* (连) ; a battalion became a *Ying* (营); the *Lu* (旅) was a brigade; the *Tuan* (团) was a regiment; a *Shi* (師) was a division; a *Jun* (军) was an army, and a *Jun-Tuan* (团) was an army group in terms of unit size.

War chariots

The war chariot formed the core of early military organization in ancient China. A Chinese war chariot was drawn by four horses and manned by three warriors of aristocratic caste. It was the command post of the army, the symbol of power and authority.

Initially, the war chariot ruled the battlefield, with the infantry in support. Infantry gained prominence during the Spring and Autumn Era due to its flexibility and the increased size in military engagements. The cavalry did not assume a significant role in the Chinese military until 307 BC when King Wuling of the Zhao kingdom adopted the nomadic warfighting technique.

During the Shang Dynasty and the early part of the ensuing Zhou Dynasty, the war chariot was the dominant arm of an army, while the infantry played an insignificant role. Infantrymen were usually slaves or servants of the charioteers. They (the infantry) took care of the feeding and maintenance of the war chariot, horses, and its crew. At the time, battles were often decided in ritualized duels between opposing chariots. With the expansion of borders beyond the plains of the Yellow River, the rough terrain and the increased sizes of military engagements brought about a fundamental transformation in the military forces. Infantry gradually gained prominence and the number of men assigned to each war-chariot grew from an initial contingent of 25 men to 75 men; some states even elevated it to 100 men.

An element of one war chariot with supporting infantry force was called a *Cheng* (乘) which was about the size of a modern armored cavalry "troop." Until the Warring States Era, a kingdom's military power was measured by the number of *Cheng* it could muster for battle.

In 541 BC, General Shun Wu of the Jin kingdom led an army against northern nomads in the mountainous region of Da-Lu. The rough terrain was a problem for the Jin war chariots. Wei Shu, a subordinate of Shun Wu, suggested the warriors abandon their chariots and fight on foot. The general agreed and appointed Wei Shu to lead the battle.

Wei Shu ordered his warriors to dismount from the chariots and form up with their infantry support troops. The aristocratic charioteers refused to join the ranks of the lower class infantrymen. Shun Wu immediately beheaded a vociferous protestor who happened to be a close friend of General Shun Wu, and that action motivated the other charioteers to dismount and form up with the infantry; the amalgamated infantry force won the battle. It was a watershed moment in Chinese military history when the infantry began to gain prominence as the dominant force on the battlefield.

Archers and crossbowmen were critical branches of the Chinese infantry. Early on, Chinese developed the system of staggered firing lines consisting of loaders, aimers and shooters to maintain a continuous volley of missiles on the opposition. A separate chapter later in this book is devoted to the development and use of crossbows in China. (See chapter on Chinese Crossbows.) Tactically, Chinese commanders formed killer teams of archers and crossbowmen to shoot at designated target(s) to ensure a priority kill. They were usually deployed to kill enemy leaders and disrupt the opposition's formations. The tactic was especially applicable in the defensive role and had a demoralizing effect on the attacking force.

Elite troops were first mentioned during the Shang dynasty. Units of royal guardsmen that protected the king's palace were called *Hu Ben* (Leaping Tigers); in latter dynasties, the term *"Hu Ben"* often became synonymous with elite fighting units. Wu Qi was the first general to establish a formal qualification system for elite soldiers (See chapter on Wu Qi — The Flawed Perfect General). The Ch'in kingdom had its own shock troops (See chapter on The Bare Head Brigade, Berserker Troops of Ancient China).

In 307 BC, King Wuling of the Zhao kingdom revolutionized Chinese land warfare by introducing *Hufuhuqi* 胡服胡骑 "Nomadic Outfits and Nomadic Riders"; he ordered his soldiers to shed their long robes for the form-fitting nomadic pants; they learned to ride and fight like the nomads. In time, his disciplined cavalry defeated the nomads and made the Zhao kingdom one of the premier powers of the time. It was the birth of Chinese cavalry.

Initially, the lack of stirrups limited the use of stabbing weapons by the cavalry. Riders were primarily armed with bows and arrows and employed as raiders, scouts, couriers and screening forces. The cavalry usually constituted less than one tenth of a kingdom's armed forces. However, by 200 BC, cavalry had surged to the fore as an important arm of the army with the appearance of independent cavalry units commanded by cavalry generals. In 202 BC, General Xiang Yu led 800 cavalrymen in a breakout attempt against his foes; he was pursued by Cavalry General Guan Ying with a force of 5,000 cavalrymen. (See chapter on The Peasant and the Warrior: The Founding of the Imperial Han Empire.)

Emperor Han Wu (157–87 BC), the seventh emperor of the Han Dynasty, was able to expand the Chinese borders by driving back the *Xiongnu* nomads, thus securing the Silk Road. He did so by maintaining a large cavalry force, especially on his western border. At times he was known to have dispatched armies of 100,000 cavalrymen to battle the *Xiongnu*. Indirectly, Western

Europe had China to thank for the invasion by the Scourge of God, because Attila the Hun and his tribesmen were descendants of the *Xiongnu* who had been driven westward by the Han cavalry.

Prior to the Warring States Era, generals rode in chariots into battle. Sometime during that era, commanders started riding horses instead of war chariots so as to gain mobility in the battlefield. In time, chariots were retired completely and duels between war chariots became duels on horsebacks.

Fights between opposing generals on horseback were rich fodder for Chinese fables. The most storied deed was "Forcing Five Gates and Slaying Six Generals" (*Guo wu guan zhan lio jiang* 过五关斩六将), where Guan Yu successfully escorted his sister-in-law to join his blood-brother Liu Bei. For his loyalty, sense of honor, and his martial feats he became known as the War God. Guan Yu's picture graces the cover of this book; he was holding his famous long knife — "Dragon Under the Moon" (青龙偃月刀) while riding his favorite steed, "The Red Rabbit." Guan Yu's "Dragon Under the Moon" weighted over 100 pounds. The heavy blade allowed the wielder to slice through the armor of the foe. Later copies of the Dragon Under the Moon were much lighter but nevertheless were accorded the name of 'Guan Dao' (Guan Yu's Knife).

Command and Control

Ancient Chinese armies had a loose command structure over the aforementioned basic unit formations. The army was under the centralized command of the emperor or the king, with small regional forces and militias in outlying areas. That was to prevent adventuresome generals from fomenting rebellions. The risk was real: the Imperial Tang Dynasty (AD 618–907) fell because its emperors entrusted large armies to generals for them to secure the frontiers. In time, those generals became powerful warlords and rebelled, culminating in the downfall of the empire.

During peacetime, local regions maintained minimal armed forces and generals had limited control over military units. Troop movements were not allowed without formal authorization from the emperor. Generals were kept at the capital, where they served as courtiers at the imperial court. In times of need, the ruler would name a courtier to take command of an army; the appointed courtier was usually, but not necessarily, a military officer. At the same time, a trusted official of the emperor was designated as the Adjutant General (Jiān jūn 监军). The Adjutant General ensured that the army commander carried out his orders and did not pose a threat to the king or the emperor. At times, generals have been known to refuse to accept the command of an army. (See Chapter on Bai Chi, the Most Successful General in Chinese History).

An order from the ruler to the general in the field was authenticated by a "Tiger Seal."

3. Tiger Seal, Shaanxi Historical Museum, Shaanxi Province, China.

The Tiger Seal was a bronze prowling tiger statue eight centimeters long with bright golden calligraphy painted on the body. The Tiger Seal was manufactured in one piece, then cut in half lengthwise. The field commander held the left half. Upon receipt of an order from the ruler, the general would match his half of the Tiger Seal with the other half from the messenger. The successful melding of the two halves of the seal authenticated the message as having come from the king/emperor.

A commander had the latitude to organize his army as he saw fit. A general in the field was attended by a group of staff officers. They served as his advisors and subordinate commanders. The general assigned a mission to a staff officer, then issued units of men to the said officer to carry out the order.

A good commander had to know the military expertise or specialty of his subordinate commanders. The system demanded close working relationships between a commander and his subordinates and allowed the commander to adapt and adjust his force to the needs of the operational environment. At the same time, it made great demands on a commander's professional expertise and situational awareness, not to mention the careful selection of his subordinate staff officers. Upon completion of a mission, the subordinate commander returned the command of his unit to the general. A general relinquished his command when he had accomplished his task, or was replaced by the ruler, or died.

As with all armies of the world, communication was a crucial part of the Chinese military organization. Smoke signals by day and flaming fires at night were used in watchtowers to give alarms on sightings of enemies. In the battlefield, couriers, drums, gongs, flags, and cannons were standard communication tools for transmitting commands. Drum beats were signals for soldiers to advance; the piercing sound of gongs could penetrate the din of battle and were sounded to withdraw or recall troops. Different colored flags or pennants were signals for pre-set instructions; and with the advent of gunpowder, cannon fire often replaced the waving flags. Kites, lanterns, whistles and signal arrows affixed with whistles were also common tools for transmitting battlefield information and commands. Western influence introduced the bugle into the Chinese military, which was heard in the Korean War.

Traditionally, Chinese soldiers were locally recruited, organized and trained as a unit with the same officers that led them into battle. Junior officers often rose through the ranks and knew their men personally. The officers' uniforms and head gear served to identify their status.

However, in modern times, the officers of the People's Liberation Army (PLA) wore the same uniform as their men with no rank differentiation. This became a problem in the Sino-Vietnamese War of 1979 when replacement officers were unable to command units because troops did not recognize their (officers) ranks, especially when young-looking officers tried to take charge of a unit. After that war, China instituted rank tabs for the PLA.

Chapter 2. Ancient Chinese Weapons and Equipment

In the West, castles were often designed as separate military base camps, whereas Chinese fortresses encompassed entire cities. The military barracks and parade grounds were located inside the city walls, with the civilian populace. Often they were a city within a city, like the Forbidden City inside Beijing.

Thus, to besiege a Chinese fortress was to attack a city and its people, and the people of the city often took part in the city's defensive effort.

The constant and continuous warfare during the Warring States Era fostered advancements in military technology and strategy.

Equipment

Traction Trebuchet

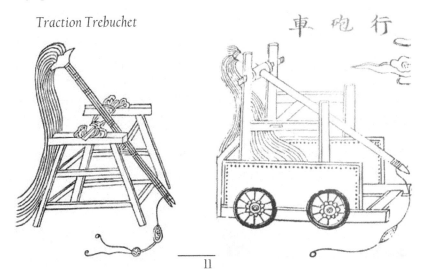

4. Standard Trebuchet, its wheeled version and the ship-borne variant. Military Encyclopedia (*Wu Jing Zong Yao*) AKA: *Complete Essentials for the Military Classics*, Song Dynasty, AD 1044.

The Chinese catapult or traction trebuchet was one of the earliest innovations in siege warfare (circa 500 BC). To fire the weapon, soldiers simply pulled on ropes attached to the short arm of a lever that had a sling mounted on the longer arm. The lever arm and the sling used the fulcrum to power the throwing of the stone or bomb at the enemy. The standard Traction Trebuchet was small and light, with a range of around 200–400 feet. An increase in altitude would extend the range of the weapon. The machine was mobile and had a shorter cycle time than the Western counterweight-powered trebuchet. Most important of all, its simplicity and light weight allowed for maximum mobility and striking power at minimal cost (for construction). It also presented a small target for counter-battery fire from the other side.

The smallest traction trebuchets could be powered by the weight and pulling force of one person using a single rope, but most were designed and sized for 15 to 45 men. The weapon was used in both the offensive and defensive modes. When it was necessary to defend a city, civilians often were drafted into servicing the weapons.

Large Traction Trebuchets had a range of up to 200 feet (30 to 61 meters) when casting weights up to 110 kg or 200 meters with lesser weights. Aside from rocks, soldiers also used trebuchets to launch bombs of lime, sulfur, and gunpowder.

5. Ancient Chinese Bombs.

The Bed Crossbow

The Bed Crossbow was the Chinese version of the ballista. It was also known as the "Eight Oxen Crossbow" because it took the equivalent strength of eight oxen to arm the machine. The earliest record mentioned Mozi, a famous pacifist of the Warring States Era, as having promoted the use of the Bed Crossbow in the defensive role.

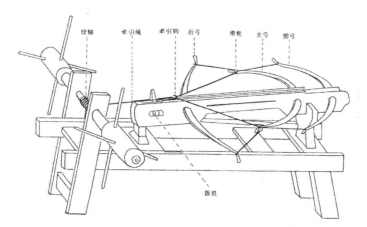

6. The Bed Crossbow

Ch'in Shih Huang Di, the First Emperor of China, sent expeditions into the Eastern Ocean to seek the elixir of eternal life. The crew returned and reported that their way was blocked by a giant fish. The First Emperor personally sailed out and killed the giant fish with a Bed Crossbow. This is probably the earliest recorded shipborne mechanical harpooning of a whale.

The Song Dynasty (AD 960–1279) developed a Bed Crossbow with a range of 1.536 kilometers that could fire giant bolts or bombs.

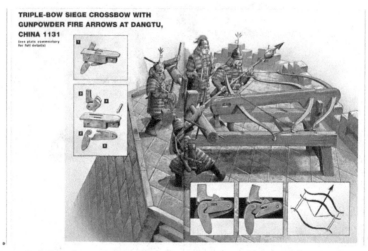

7. Bed Crossbow in the defense, firing explosive arrows.

Although it was initially conceived as a defensive weapon, due to its size and weight, Chinese generals managed to put the Bed Crossbow into offensive use. An unusual offensive employment was to line up a phalanx of the machines and fire "Stepping Arrows" at the city wall. The attacking soldiers could then climb the Stepping Arrows impaled in the city wall to breach its defenses.

The Nest Cart

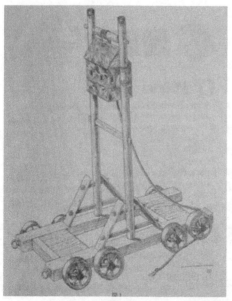

8. The Nest Cart

The Nest Cart was a simple tree house on wheels used to observe and report on enemy activities. The ropes raised and lowered the nest on the supporting framework.

The Cloud Ladder

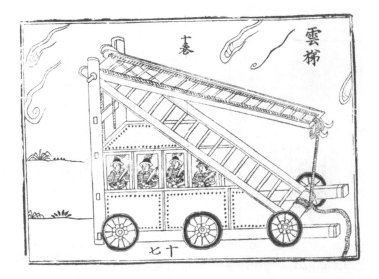

9. The Cloud Ladder, Military Encyclopedia

The Cloud Ladder was a folding ladder on wheels. Once the cart was in position, men pulled the rope that ran under the cart and lifted the upper portion of the ladder into place, against the defender's wall, with the hooks latched onto the parapet. Soldiers were protected in the cart until it was time to scale the ladder.

Pontoon Bridge

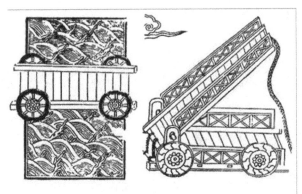

10. Pontoon Bridge, Military Encyclopedia

The Pontoon Bridge was very much like the Cloud Ladder and worked like a modern military pontoon bridge to span a moat.

Defensive Equipment

Flying Hook, Wolf Fang Smasher

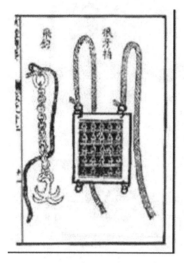

11. The Flying Hook and the Wolf Fang Smasher, Military Encyclopedia

The *Fei Go* (Flying Hook), depicted at left, was a four-pronged hook attached at the end of a chain and long rope. The defensive forces would throw it down from the city wall to catch a siege ladder or tower and then pull (using sheer muscle power or a winch) to topple the attacker's equipment.

The *Lang Ya Pai* (Wolf Fang Smasher), depicted to the right of the *Fei Go*, was a large, heavy board affixed with sharp blades. At the four corners of the board were rings attached to ropes. The ropes were tied together to a longer rope connected to a pulley atop the wall. Defenders dropped the *Lang Ya Pai* on top of attackers, then used the pulley to retrieve the weapon for reuse.

The Witches' Thunder

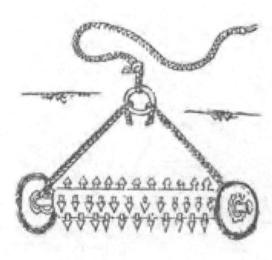

12. The Witches' Thunder, Military Encyclopedia

The *Yeh Cha Lei* 夜叉雷 (Witches' Thunder) was a large, heavy log with metal spikes across its length. It looked like a giant spiked rolling pin with ropes attached to both ends. It was used as a companion weapon to the *Lang Ya Pai* and was deployed in a similar manner.

The Door Jammer

13. The Door Jammer

The Door Jammer was a two-wheeled cart with sharp blades mounted across its face. It was used to plug breaches in defensive positions, usually at gateways, and where the narrow alleys intersected within the tight confines of the cities. It was simple, easy to manufacture, highly mobile and could be made to fit the size of the defensive positions. Pushed along by defenders, it would slow the advance of attackers. And as a last resort, it could be set on fire to block the lanes and delay enemy advances.

Gun Powder Weapons

Initially, gunpowder was only used for sending signals. Its use was quickly expanded and rockets were devised for signaling and later as weapons. Still later, simple cannons came into existence.

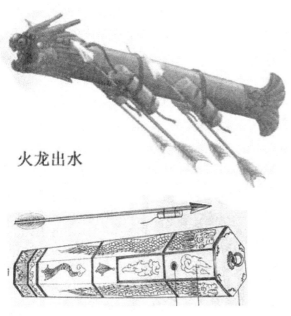

火龙出水

14. The Fire Dragon

The Fire Dragon was a naval weapon that flew at enemy ships while firing explosive rockets from its mouth.

15. The Long Snake Arrow Box

The Long Snake Arrow Box was the land-based version of the Fire Dragon. Each box was packed with 40 rockets. Numerous boxes were mounted together on a cart for firing at the enemy. It was like an early version of the multiple rocket launcher.

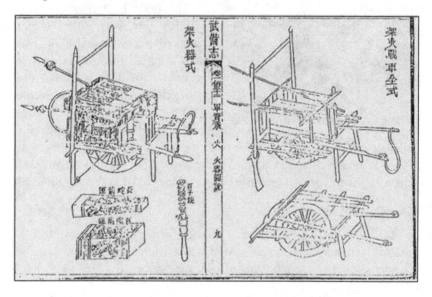

16. The Long Snake Arrow Box and the mounting carts, Military Encyclopedia. Note the empty and collapsed transport platforms in the traveling position.

17. The Thunder Fire Ball, Military Encyclopedia

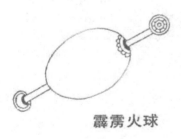

霹雳火球

The Thunder Fire Ball was an early version of a grenade. It consisted of a ball of gunpowder, broken pottery and metal shards wrapped around a tube of bamboo that was about one and a half inch in diameter, with the two ends of the bamboo protruding from the ball. The fuse for the grenade went in one end of the tube; the grenadier would hold the other end of the bamboo, light the fuse, then toss it at the enemy. Weight, transportation, maintenance and storage requirements usually limited its usage to the defensive role.

There are also records of ancient Chinese land and maritime mines made with gun powder inside, but information on their usage and reliability is too scarce to warrant detailed analysis.

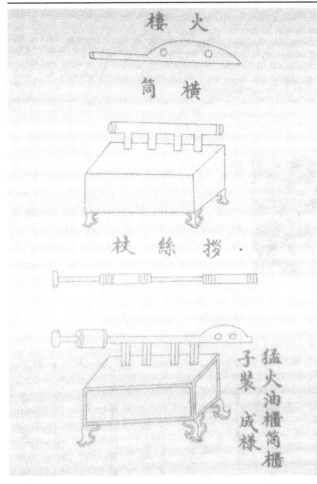

18. The Flame Thrower, Military Encyclopedia

The Chinese flamethrower was a double-piston pump machine comprised of a rectangular fuel container with a brass piston tube on top. A soldier pulled the piston back to draw fuel from the fuel reservoir, then pushed the fuel out over a pilot light to spray the flaming liquid. The size, weight, and fuel supply requirements limited it predominantly to the defensive role, and the lack of wheels also indicates its defensive nature.

Personal Weapons

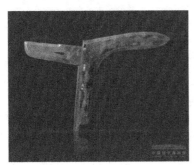

19. The Dagger Ax (*Ge*) head, National Museum of China

Ge (戈), the Dagger Ax, evolved from the farmer's sickle. The earliest *ge* artifact dates from the Shang Dynasty, about 1500 BC. It was once considered the king of weapons and the weapon of kings.

Kings used the *ge* in battle and were buried with jade-carved *ge* in their tombs. A standard *ge* could be 14 to 18 feet in length, which indicated its standard use as a chariot warfare weapon. Its length allowed the warrior to cut, slash and hook the enemy from the opposing war chariot. The greatest threat posed by the *ge* was not the sharp point of the ax but the cutting edge below the blade, used like a scythe to hook the foe from behind after the initial strike.

20. Short *Ge*

Infantry used the standard *ge* and the short *ge* in battle. The short *ge* was handy as a single-hand weapon, whereas it required two hands to use the standard *ge* effectively. Later, enterprising armorers added a spear tip to the *ge* and created the *ji* (戟), which allowed a more lethal thrust against the enemy.

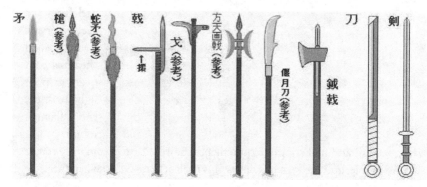

21. Lance Spear Snake-Lance Ji Ge Ji Guan-Dao Ji Knife Sword

Above is a small sample of common individual close-combat weapons used by ancient Chinese armies. Notice the various versions of the *ji* (#4, #6, and #8). The red horse hairs bunched at the base of some lance and spear blades (#2 and #3) were twirled during thrusting of the weapon. The hairs flared out to confuse the enemy and at the same time served to shield the wielder from blood sprayed after the weapon struck the target. The aforementioned Guan-Dao (#7) was a heavy cavalry weapon; the heavy blade could cut through horse, armor, and man with one stroke. Soldiers used the knife (#9) or the sword (#10) for combat in close quarters; the knife had only one cutting edge, whereas the sword was double-edged. Officers wore swords only. Aristocrats wore swords as a symbol of rank and nobility. The longer the sword, the higher the rank of the wearer.

Longbows and crossbows were well developed in ancient China; they were formidable arms. Expert archers were well respected. During the Spring and Autumn Era, a man named Yang You-Ji shot 100 arrows at a stand of willow trees from 100 paces. Each of the arrows pierced a willow leaf, thus giving birth to the expression of "Piercing willows at 100 paces" to describe the skill of an expert marksman. The draw of a bow was measured in stone weights, where one stone weight (*Dan* 石) equals about 30 pounds, roughly double the British "stone." Most archers pulled three-stone bows, but some warriors were known to have pulled ten-stone bows.

Bodkin pointed arrowheads were used during the Warring States Era, 1,500 years before their appearance in Europe. It was the standard arrow used by archers of the Ch'in kingdom.

22. Bodkin arrowheads unearthed at the Chang-Ping battle site, scene of the greatest military disaster in ancient history; over half a million men are said to have perished in the campaign (262–260 BC). See chapter on Bai Chi, the Most Successful General in Chinese History.

A separate chapter is devoted to Crossbows.

Personal Protective Equipment

Significantly, the Chinese did not devote as much effort to the development of personal protective equipment as they did to offensive gear. Helmets were usually simple leather and cloth affairs. Officers wore elaborately decorated metal helmets that left the face uncovered. No full-faced helmets like those used by ancient Greeks or medieval European knights were ever seen in China.

Common soldiers used rattan or leather-embossed wooden shields, but not officers, and a general was never depicted with a shield. The shield was considered cumbersome and would appear cowardly if used by officers. This points to a strategic emphasis on mobility and maneuverability in military planning and operations. Aside from arrogance and pride, officers wanted to demonstrate their fearlessness to the enemy and their own troops.

China shunned the heavy-plate body armor of European medieval knights. Chinese armors were generally simple affairs of boiled leather. Officers wore more complex leather and lacquer armor that covered the front, back, limbs and the neck; some officers wore round metal discs that protected the heart and the back. The key was flexibility for the user. Historical records show numerous incidents where commanders were unhorsed in combat but were able to quickly remount and continue the fight. This demonstrates the Chinese preference for flexible armor that did not impede mobility.

The Ch'in army of the Warring States Era had "Bare Head Brigades" where men went into battle wearing only battle tunics, with neither armor nor helmet; some men even fought bare-chested.

Chapter 3. Strategic Cultural Thinking

"A thousand soldiers are easy to find; an able general is difficult to acquire." Said proverb pointed to the importance of a capable commander as the most decisive factor in winning wars.

Traditionally, Chinese rulers devoted great efforts to seeking the finest generals; at the same time, they went to great lengths to remove or deprive their enemies of a great general or talented individual. In ancient times, a king or emperor would request rather than order an able soldier to take command of an army; and there were rare occasions where individuals refused the offer to command an army.

The command of an army is a double-edged sword. Time and distance made communications difficult; thus, once in command, a general in the field held extraordinary powers. By tradition, a commander in a campaign was not obliged to obey every order received from his ruler, because the commander had a better appreciation of the tactical situation and environment. Of course, afterward, the general could lose his head, whether his judgment proved correct or otherwise. All of this made the choice of a commander extremely important.

"Know thy enemy and know thyself; you shall persevere in all your battles." The famous quote from Sun Tzu points to the importance of information. Intelligence networks were extensively used to collect information, fabricate misinformation/disinformation, create misdirection and conduct assassinations.

"A country that did not collect intelligence information on its enemies and even its allies did so at its own peril. Who knew when friends became foes?" Aside from gathering military-related information, spies gathered biographic data, professional backgrounds, personal habits, and close relationships of enemy commanders and political leaders.

Intelligence or information gathering was a fundamental part of the Chinese military culture. Sun Tzu devoted a whole chapter of his treatise to the use of spies. He divided the espionage system into five categories: local informants; recruited assets; double agents; suicide spies (agents provocateurs); and penetration agents.

Local informants provided general area knowledge of the targeted region. Recruited assets were officials of the targeted country. Double agents were spies of the enemy recruited for your own use. Suicide spies were people you sent to provide false information to induce the opposition into making a wrong decision. They were suicide spies because they were not expected to survive their missions. Penetration agents were men sent into the enemy camp to bring back crucial information or accomplish a specific task.

Chinese leader used spies to recruit talented men from foreign countries to serve the king or the emperor. A good modern example was the case of Qian Xuesen (钱学森, 11 December 1911–31 October 2009; AKA: H. S. Tsien). Qian was a leading US expert on missile and space technology, and one of the three founders of the Jet Propulsion Laboratory, Caltech. The US Space Shuttle was based in part on Qian's original design.

Qian's father-in-law was a close confidant and advisor to Generalissimo Chiang Kai-Shek, leader of the Chinese Nationalist Party (the *Kuomintang*) and a staunch opponent of Communist China; therefore, there was no reason for Qian to favor the Communist Party of China. However, the FBI came across an American Communist Party document with Qian's name on it. The document caused the revocation of Qian's US intelligence security clearance, and Qian lost his job. Chairman Mao Zedong wrote a personal letter and invited Qian to return to China, and that was how Qian became the father of Chinese rocketry and missiles. There was no evidence of Chinese skullduggery, but the fortuitous appearance of the American Communist Party document certainly facilitated China's acquisition of a leading rocket expert from the US.

Chinese people are pragmatists; they will use anything at hand to achieve their goal. Weather, terrain, people, and forces of nature are mere tools of battle. Water, fire, and livestock are often useful to a commander. History provides ample examples of Chinese generals employing the above items to achieve victory.

Trench warfare and tunneling have been common tactics since ancient times. Attackers dug trenches and tunnels to penetrate the defenders' walled enclosures. Defenders would counter tunnel to detect enemy diggings, and this concurrently weakened the subterranean structure of the ground so that it might collapse under the weight of the attackers' siege engines. The attackers' equipment might get stuck in a rut, tilt, or tip over, becoming more vulnerable to the defenders' trebuchets and flame weapons.

Pragmatic Chinese espionage organizations had no qualms regarding co-opting criminal groups. There was ample evidence of symbiotic relationships between the Chinese triads, law enforcement agencies, and the intelligence services. The aforementioned Chiang Kai-Shek was a member of the *Qingbang* (Green Society Triad). In 1927, with the assistance of the Green Society, he initiated the purge of the Chinese Communist Party in Shanghai which culminated in the Long March. The Chinese Communist Party would have been wiped out but for Japan's untimely invasion of China, which forced a Nationalist rapprochement with the Communist Party, and the rest is history.

Human psychology was and still is one of the favorite means to deceive and outwit the enemy. Psychological warfare has had close to 3,000 years of history in China. Many Korean War veterans remembered Chinese propaganda broadcasts on the battlefield and the brainwashing of prisoners.

The Strategy of Beauties (美人計 *Mei Ren Ji*) referred to the employment of sex to achieve the desired goal. Historically, Chinese strategists often presented beautiful women as gifts to the opposition leader. The women were intended to distract the enemies and interfere with their job performance. The women also spied on the opposition, and at times were used to destroy a man's reputation, thus making him a liability for his people. Finally, women could persuade the opponent to be friendlier to the spymaster's kingdom.

A Chinese general would use psychology not only to defeat the enemy but also to motivate his own men in battle. In World War II, an innovative Chinese general learned that many of his young soldiers had never seen a naked woman and, with the coming battle, probably never would. The normally highly moral and proper commander decided to show a pornographic movie to his men. The ploy endeared him to the troops and raised their morale for the coming battle.

Western strategists have stressed the importance of the 'offense' — "Riding to the Sound of the Gun." Chinese strategists often preferred patience, 以逸待劳 *Yi Yi Dai Lao* (Wait and rest, then fight those who are tired). Whenever possible, Chinese generals chose the time and place of battle and let the enemy come to them. An army on the march required supplies and was more vulnerable to attack than a stationary or hidden force. A well-rested army faced by an enemy that was tired from a long march had a better chance at victory.

An army fights on its stomach; Chinese generals favor attacks on enemy supply lines and supply depots because those are soft targets. Captured goods could supply the victor and in addition provided information on the enemy.

"Victory without the use of force is the best form of strategy." War was an extension of diplomacy. Chinese leaders employed asymmetric warfare as a matter of course. A Chinese strategist would seek to attain his goal through diplomacy before resorting to force, as amply described in later chapters. False flag operations and *agents provocateurs* to incite conflict between foreign foes had been common staples of Chinese diplomacy and strategy since ancient times. Even during the midst of a campaign, generals would attempt to persuade allies of the opposition to change sides.

In the early 20th century, Huang Pu Military Academy, the Chinese counterpart to the US Military Academy at West Point, produced numerous officers that later commanded armies on both sides of the post-WWII Chinese Civil War (1945–1949). Included were 32 Communist Chinese generals; the most notable Communist alumni of Huang Pu were Marshals Lin Biao 林彪, Xu Xian Qian 徐向前, Nie Rong Ji 聂荣臻 and Ye Jian Ying 叶剑英. During the said Chinese Civil War, there were often cross-line communications between former Huang Pu classmates, not unlike the West Point graduates of American Civil War era. Except, in the case of China, many Nationalist (*Kuomintang*) generals were persuaded to defect with their armies to join their Communist classmates.

In a siege, a Chinese attacker often left the defenders an escape route under the axiom that soldiers with a chance to escape might not fight as hard and might be induced into desertion, and desertion can be infectious in an army. In addition, an enemy in retreat is more vulnerable, not to mention the psychological effect it has on other enemy forces. Disorganized troops on the run would also be more liable to surrender than fight. Finally, the open route into the besieged area allowed spies to enter and conduct espionage.

It should be noted that a Chinese commander would not shy away from the use of force to achieve a political end. In 1950, the Chinese Communist Party (CCP) had just won the civil war and needed to consolidate its power. At the time, there were over a million ex-Nationalist troops in mainland China. With Chiang Kai-Shek in Taiwan, those former Nationalist soldiers posed a significant threat to the CCP. Mao Tze-Tung sent a large number of the ex-Nationalist soldiers to fight in the Korean War. The maneuver fanned nationalistic fervor and consolidated his political power, while at the same time it eliminated a potential security threat. It also paid off a political favor to Moscow and gained global renown for advancing the course of international communism.

In 1979, Deng Xiao-Ping met opposition from his senior military commanders when he tried to reform and modernize the People's Liberation

Army (PLA). He used the Sino-Vietnamese War to teach the Old Guard a lesson about the need for modernization and military reform. The bloody nose the PLA suffered in that war brought the Chinese military leadership into line for Deng.

Chinese often use history as a guide to their decisions and actions. The following chapters will introduce some famous Chinese leaders and significant battles that exemplify Chinese warfare. They are the people and battles that modern Chinese commanders study. They demonstrate how Chinese generals apply the lessons from their forefathers. As you will see, Chinese strategists emphasize the importance of Speed, Stealth and most importantly, Psychology.

> "It is not enough to know how the enemy thinks. A good strategist tries to make the enemy think and do things the way he wishes them to think and do."

Chapter 4. The Cultural Paradigm

The concept of "relationships" is arguably the most important aspect of Chinese society that remains unfamiliar to most foreigners. It governs the daily lives of every Chinese person and relates to everything from gods, ancestors, rulers, and employers to family members, friends, and teachers. Relationships are factors for consideration not only between people but also among businesses and between nations.

To the Chinese, the country, the society and the clan always come before the self. This is the reason why a person's family name is placed before the given name. Chinese people will provide different answers to the question, "Where are you from?" In answering to a foreigner, they will cite their place of birth or residence; however, to fellow Chinese person, the reply will list the origin of the speaker's ancestry. For example, my father's forebears were from Fu-Zhou city, Fujian Province of China. I was born in Taipei, Taiwan, grew up in New York City, and lived in Fredericksburg, Virginia, USA. To a foreigner, I would be a Taiwan-born Chinese person living in America. But to the Chinese, I am a Fu-Zhou person, and the same answer applies to my children and my son's children.

An individual's given name could also reveal his or her generational rank within a clan; often individuals of the same generation in a clan will have the same middle name. Such names are set out for each clan, in a given region, by a "generational poem" that was created by the senior members of a family when a new lineage was started. In the case of the present author, my brothers and I have "Tzu" as our middle names, and my children and their cousin have "Fu" as their middle names. This way, members of a distant but related family can identify a person's social standing within the clan by his or her name, and so they can address that person with the appropriate relational title.

Within communities, neighborhoods are organized into block security systems to help and protect each other. The block leader is usually responsible for harmony and security throughout the block. In ancient times, a person had to report any illegal activity by his neighbor(s). One person's crime could result in punishment for the entire block. Refusal to report a crime constituted aiding and abetting; so good harmonious relationships between neighbors were of paramount importance.

The relationship between a superior and a subordinate can be, at times, rigid and unforgiving. In ancient times, an emperor's command for a subordinate to commit suicide would be obeyed without question. In 210 BC, the Crown Prince of the First Emperor committed suicide upon receipt of an imperial order to take his own life. The order was forged, but the Crown Prince obediently slit his own throat. His death started the downfall of the Ch'in Dynasty, the first imperial dynasty of China.

A father is responsible for the care of his children. He owns his children's lives and can give them away to repay a debt or even order their death. A son or daughter is obligated to obey the parent. The exception to the rule applies when a daughter gets married; then she belongs to the husband's family. Since the bride's family is losing a daughter, the groom's family foots the bill for the wedding banquet.

A son is always expected to repay his late father's debts, whether monetary or metaphysical. Courtiers of the imperial eras were given yearlong bereavement leaves on the passing of a parent, and it was not unusual for a person to observe a three-year period of bereavement to honor his parents' passing.

A teacher/mentor holds significant influence over the life of a student/subordinate. These relationships may extend beyond the school and work environment. A letter of recommendation or sponsorship from a senior can jump start a person onto a path of success; of course, the kindness and generosity are expected to be repaid when the situation arises. Colleagues look after the welfare and career of each other's scions. However, sponsorships are not lightly given; should the recipient of the largesse commit an error or misdeed, the sponsor of the miscreant will be responsible and at times could be punished for misjudging his character.

Under imperial regimes, punishments for certain crimes were levied against an entire family or clan and their social relations. Parents and teachers of "social outcasts" were often ostracized and despised; during the Song Dynasty (AD 960–1279), many people changed their family name from

"Qin" to another to avoid any appearance of association with Qin Gui, the corrupt official that murdered the national hero Yueh Fei.

Relationships between friends are multi-tiered, depending on the type and level of the friendship. Once a bond is established, the friendship can transcend family ties. Chinese history is replete with tales where a man sacrificed his all, to include his own child, to protect the last surviving heir of a friend.

The most frequently-cited relationship of lore was the brotherly love and loyalty between Liu Bei, Guan Gong, and Zhang Fei. They were the heroes of the Romance of the Three Kingdoms. Guan Gong refused riches and honor and risked death to remain loyal to his sworn brother Liu Bei. For his unswerving loyalty and his military prowess, the Chinese revered Guan Gong as the War God of the land. To this day, every major Chinese city has temples honoring Guan Gong. His icons or statues decorate many households, and most Chinese restaurants and shops keep a small shrine with candles and incense to honor Guan Gong. He is usually depicted as the tall red-faced warrior with a long flowing black beard and an eight-foot-long knife (the one that was named after him — Guan Dao). Admittedly, these are extreme circumstances, but they are the ideals that Chinese admire and respect; they are also examples for educating and instilling moral values into the minds of the young.

Chinese relationships are not limited to the living. For the Chinese, a person who accomplishes exceptional deeds of valor or greatness could become a god, with people offering sacrifices and paying homage long beyond his or her passing. Prominent examples are Confucius (God of Teaching), the aforementioned Guan Gong (War God) and Lao Tzu (the founder of Daoism). This explains the profusion of temples and pagodas honoring thousands of local deities that dotted the Chinese landscape. Confucius was revered for his literary and philosophical contributions to the people; Guan Gong was deified for his extreme loyalty to his brother, the king; and Lao Tzu became a god due to his philosophical teaching which stressed the oneness with nature.

On the opposite extreme, vengeance and retribution also reached into the beyond. In 506 BC, Wu Tze She accompanied Sun Tzu in defeating the Chu kingdom. Wu Tze She's father and brother were murdered by King Ping of the Chu kingdom, so after Wu Tze She captured the Chu capital of Ying. He dug up King Ping's grave and flailed the corpse, then burned it to ashes and scattered them into a lake. To die with a dismembered body and without a proper funeral was an ultimate insult.

China considered itself a nation of rituals and etiquette (礼仪之邦 Li Yi Zhi Bang). The government treated other countries like neighbors in a world community, and traditional ties were factors for consideration. This would explain China's unwavering supportive position on North Korea. Their relationship grows out of a 2,000-year-old friendship, and one does not readily abandon old relationships.

By the same token, Chinese people hold a generally favorable view of the U.S.; this is due to several reasons. First, after China was obliged to pay reparations to the US after the Boxer Rebellion (1899–1901), the U.S. Congress authorized the use of part of that money to set up a scholarship for Chinese students (the Boxer Rebellion Indemnity Scholarship to train Chinese scholars in the U.S.); second, the United States played a role in saving China from Japan in World War II. The Chinese do not forget acts of kindness.

Chinese tend to take history lessons to heart. "History does not repeat itself; stupid people repeat history because they didn't take the time to learn from it." In 200 BC, Liu Bang, the founder of the Han Dynasty, was besieged and humiliated by the nomadic cavalry of *Xiong Nu* and had to sue for peace with annual tributes of women and gold. For the next seventy years, Han emperors continued the appeasement policy while they built up their cavalry. When they were ready, they drove the *Xiong Nu* out of Asia; the *Xiong Nu* retreated westward and became the forefathers of Attila the Hun. As can be seen, Chinese long range plans may extend over generations.

East versus West: Faced with a problem, Westerners prefer a quick-fix "fast food" resolution, while the Chinese will take time to analyze the problem, like a leisurely banquet, before they settle on a course of action. Westerners like things clear cut, in black and white, while the Chinese favor different shades of gray so as to allow for wiggle room. Westerners value individual freedom, while the Chinese submerge individualism for tranquility and the greater good. Western societies tend to prefer separation of state, military and economic infrastructures to avoid "conflict of interests." Chinese pragmatism and heavy reliance on relationships often leads to concentrating political, military and economic powers in an individual(s), even though this can provide a rich breeding ground for corruption and nepotism.

CHAPTER 5. SIX ARTS, THE MAKING OF A KNIGHT

The Six Arts — Rituals, Music, Archery, Chariotry, Books, and Numbers

In ancient China, beginning from the Zhou Dynasty, aristocrats trained their sons to master the skills necessary for entry into the ranks of gentlemen (*Jun Zi* 君子) or knights. In the process, they created the Chinese "Whole Man" concept.

The set of skills, collectively known as the Six Arts, were Rituals, Music, Archery, Chariotry, Books, and Numbers. The goal was to produce a corps of capable men who were ethically minded and of high moral character. These men were to help the king govern the nation. Men who excelled in the Six Arts were considered as having reached a state of idealism, able to hold senior ministerial posts and command armies.

However, there was no institutionalized methodology nor were there standards for training the aristocratic youths. Everything depended on the resources of the individual household, the quality of the teachers and the intelligence of the students. There was not even a rule on the age requirement for the commencement of training in the Six Arts, not to mention a formalized system for evaluation of trainees.

Upon reaching the age of twenty, a young man was assumed to have acquired all the skills necessary in the Six Arts. At the crowning ceremony (*Guan Li* 冠礼), he was granted the right to wear the bejeweled hair clasp, a symbol of maturity with the rank of a Knight (*Jun Zi* 君子).

Training in the Art of Rituals consisted of learning about law, ethics, and the proper conduct of numerous ceremonial rites befitting specific occasions. The purpose of Rituals was to produce able leaders of high moral character who could command the respect of the people, govern the land and lead the subjects in sacrificial offerings, prayers and, most importantly, communicate with the gods and ancestors. At the same time, a knight also must know the proper honors to render guests and foreign dignitaries at formal encounters so as not to embarrass or insult the guest(s) — unless it was intended so.

The Art of Music taught the young men to sing, project their voices with poise and authority, create poetry, dance and play musical instruments. The training was aimed at developing sophisticated minds capable of looking beyond daily mundane issues. A leader had to be a man of superior character and foresight, able to think with a creative and critical mind. At the advanced training stage, dancing lessons entailed performances with shields and swords, thus becoming a form of exercise and an instrument for the physical development of a man into a warrior.

The Art of Archery was a ritualized and demanding martial skill that required the archer to shoot arrows with power and speed. A man had to be able to fire multiple arrows in rapid succession, with each shot hitting the mark. It also specified a ceremonial courteous ceding of advantages to the king when shooting in the company of the ruler, such as allowing the king to shoot first and at a closer range to the target. It would not be proper to outperform a king on the archery range.

The Art of Charioteer involved more than the mere driving of a horse-drawn carriage. The chariot served as the command post of a military leader on the battlefield. The steering of a chariot symbolized acquisition of leadership skills necessary to command armies in battle. Individuals had to learn the intricacies of military organizations, tactics, troop movement and the deployment of soldiers into various combat formations to meet the needs of the terrain and field environment.

Ancient Chinese war chariots were drawn by four horses and manned with a crew of three warrior knights — the troop commander/driver in the center, the archer to the left, and the guard/halberd bearer on the right. Each chariot usually had an escort contingent of seventy-two infantrymen. When a king or ruler took to the field, he rode in the center of the chariot. The troop commander/driver shifted to the left position and drove the chariot from that location, while the archer was displaced; and the guard/halberd bearer position was taken by the best warrior of the land, to protect the king/ruler.

In ancient times, a nation's military power was not measured by the number of men it could field but by the number of chariots it could muster for battle. Sending a thousand chariots into battle meant dispatching an army of 75,000 men.

Before and during the early phase of the Spring and Autumn Era, battles often were ritualized affairs, commencing with dueling war chariots, not unlike the jousting contests of medieval knights in Europe. A challenge for battle would be issued and accepted. At the appointed time and place, two generals or kings in their respective chariots would charge at each other with the chariots' archers firing arrows from a distance. As the warriors closed with each other, halberd (ji) bearers would take swings at the foes with their four-meter long poleaxes. After each pass, assuming no serious damage had resulted from the encounter, the chariots would turn around and charge again. The exchange would continue until one side became a casualty or decided to abandon the field, at which time the rest of the army would either charge forward or run away.

The Art of Books entailed the study of history, philosophy, literature, and calligraphy. The Chinese believed that a person's character could be revealed through his handwriting. Training to be a good calligrapher served to develop and refine one's inner soul. Books enabled individuals to learn from the examples of their ancestors. That was especially important because the Chinese always looked to the past for guidance in their decisions for the present and the future.

The Art of Numbers included mathematics, astronomy, astrology, and forecasting for making predictions. It trained the mind in the planning of strategy and tactics for use in social, political and military arenas. It opened mental paths for thinking ahead and prepared an individual to deal with unexpected circumstances.

The extensive time, financial resources and availability of capable teachers necessary for training in the Six Arts limited the practice to the realm of aristocrats. Even then, the final products were often not up to par, forcing rulers to seek able men from outside their kingdoms. Eventually, changes in the political and military environment and the demand for capable courtiers forced the relaxation of the Six Arts training regimen. They were pared down to concentrate on Books with reduced emphasis on other skills. Commoners were then able to train in the Art of Books and then enter the services of lords and kings.

During the latter part of the Spring and Autumn Era and the ensuing Warring States Era (476–221 BC), well-learned men from all tiers of society were accepted into the ranks of courtiers because kings and rulers needed talented men to serve in their courts. Conversely, educated and talented men sought enlightened rulers for opportunities to demonstrate their (courtier) skills and apply their theories, and thus gain fame and fortune. The best-known example of a successful knight was Sun Tzu, who convinced King He Lu of the Wu kingdom to hire him as the Commander of the Wu army and subsequently went on to defeat the more powerful Chu kingdom. His legacy was *The Art of War*, the earliest and most studied treatise on the conduct of warfare.

A less well known but equally successful knight was Confucius. Everyone knew him as a scholar, philosopher, and teacher. Few people outside of China were aware of his talent as an accomplished musician and administrator; however, the least known fact was that Confucius was also a military leader.

In 500 BC, Confucius escorted Duke Wen of the Lu state to a summit meeting with Duke Jing of the Qi state. Aware of the avaricious nature of the opposition, Duke Jing, Confucius insisted that Duke Wen bring along a large military escort. At the Jiagu Mountain meeting site, Confucius was proven correct in his precautions as Lu army scouts reported that Duke Jing had brought a large army to the summit. Confucius placed his army on alert status and summoned an additional force of three hundred war chariots to be stationed ten *li* away (five km) from Jiagu Mountain.

At the summit, three hundred Qi warriors dressed as dancers performed for the guests. It was an obvious attempt to intimidate and then kidnap Duke Wen. Confucius confronted Duke Jing and forced the duke to retire the dancers and then ordered Lu officers to behead the two leaders of the Qi dancing troupes for disrespectful behavior to a sovereign ruler. Faced with the forceful response from Confucius, Duke Jing retreated in disgrace from the summit and Confucius' military deployments prevented the Qi army from executing its planned attack against Duke Wen.

Afterward, as a gesture of apology for his discourtesy at the summit meeting, Duke Jing of Qi returned to Duke Wen all the territory that the Qi nation had previously taken from the Lu kingdom.

Confucius' governance turned the Lu kingdom into a law abiding and powerful nation, which became a major concern to Duke Jing's ambitious goals. The duke resorted to subterfuge to accomplish what he had failed to do via diplomacy or force of arms; he sent Duke Wen fifteen beautiful women as gifts. The women captured Duke Wen's attention, and the ruler lost interest in the affairs of the state.

Confucius tried but failed to persuade Duke Wen to pay more attention to his duties as the head of state. In despair, Confucius resigned and left the Lu nation. Subsequently, the deteriorated Lu state was conquered by the powerful Chu nation.

The Six Arts system trained a corps of ethical and capable leaders to serve as diplomats, administrators, and generals that governed and protected the kingdoms. Theoretically, each knight was qualified in both civil and military capacity for his lord or king.

In time, the tradition of training in the Art of Books as a means to attain prominence evolved into the Imperial examination system designed to gain entry as Mandarin officials for Chinese emperors. To this date, Chinese governments in China and Taiwan both practice the examination system for hiring civil servants. Due to the widespread Chinese cultural influence, variations of the Chinese civil service examination systems can also be found in many Asian countries.

The well-recognized Chinese desire for education and learning as a path to success traces its origin to the Six Arts of a Chinese Knight. The legacy of the Six Arts was best depicted by Guan Yu, the War God of Chinese folklore; he was frequently seen reading a book, instead of wielding his weapon, the three-meter long large bladed knife — *Guan Dao*, which was named after him.

The legacy of the Six Arts is the Chinese ideal of The Whole Man concept (Gentleman-君子) — a well-educated, humble but capable man of high morals, and ethical in character. The term *Jun* (君), depending on its usage, has many meanings; it can mean a King, a Knight or Mister when addressing a male person.

23. Statue of Guan Yu the
War God of China reading
a book atop a mountain in
Taiwan. Photo by Fred Hsu

CHAPTER 6. SAN YANG, THE IRON CHANCELLOR, ARCHITECT OF IMPERIAL CHINA

If there were just one person that could be credited as the architect who created China as a nation, San Yang (395–338 BC) would be that man. His political, economic, and military policies enabled the Ch'in kingdom to rise from a barbaric backwater state to a first rate power that ultimately conquered the other kingdoms to create the Imperial Ch'in Empire, which subsequently evolved into the China of today.

However, San Yang's merciless disciplinarian policies created many enemies, which ultimately led to his demise.

24. San Yang

* * *

Born an aristocrat, San Yang was originally known as Way Yang, because he was from a minor kingdom named Way. Initially, San Yang served the Prime Minister of the powerful Wei kingdom. The Prime Minister recognized the exceptional talent in the young man but did not promote him for fear that he would excel and overshadow the Prime Minister's position.

However, on his deathbed, the Prime Minister recommended Way Yang to King Hui, ruler of the Wei nation, to be the next Prime Minister. But if the king did not want to use Way Yang, he advised, then he should be killed to prevent him from serving another kingdom.

After the king returned to the palace, the Prime Minister summoned Way Yang and told him, "I just recommended you to the king for the position of the prime minister. I also told the king that if he does not use you, he should kill you. He did not appear willing to follow my advice." He then slowly lifted a feeble hand and pointed to a sack by the foot of the bed, "Therefore, I suggest you take this sack of gold and leave before the king sends his henchmen to kill you."

Way Yang shook his head in disagreement, "If the king did not listen to your suggestion to employ me, why would he heed your words to kill me?" As predicted, after the prime minister died, the king did not appoint Yang to replace the courtier but neither did he order Yang killed.

* * *

In 361 BC, Duke Xiao, ruler of the Ch'in State, issued a summons for men of talent. Yang jumped at the opportunity and traveled to Dong-Yang, the capital of the Ch'in kingdom. He entered the service of the courtier Jing Jian, and sought Jing's sponsorship for a meeting with Duke Xiao.

In 358 BC, with the help of his patron, Yang had four interviews with the Duke. At the first two meetings, Yang talked about governance via the Dao of Kings, in the traditions of the ancient sage kings of the land, and the Dao of the Benevolent Ruler, in the Confucian ideals of humanity and humility.

The Duke was not impressed by Yang's presentations and almost dozed off. Yang realized the duke did not want to be a mere ruler; he wished to be a conqueror. At the third interview, Yang introduced the Dao of the Dominant Ruler that emphasized war preparations and conquests. This time, his ideas received the duke's full attention. At the fourth audience, Yang delineated the path to a strong nation through agrarian, military and social reforms.

Yang won the confidence of the Duke and received the appointment of Chancellor of the Realm.

Yang felt that before he implemented his new policies, he needed to gain the trust of the people in their government. He placed a ten-foot long pole at the south gate of the city with a royal proclamation, "Any person that moves the pole to the north gate of the city shall receive ten pieces of gold." But not one person bothered to take up the challenge.

Yang then increased the reward to fifty pieces of gold. Finally, one man took up the offer and moved the post to the north gate. Yang immediately gave him the promised fifty pieces of gold. The stunt established the credibility of the government and in 356 BC Yang published his first new set of laws for the realm:

1. Every citizen had to have an identity chit. Inns were not allowed to accept customers without an identity chit. People without identity chits would be treated as criminals and punished as such; innkeepers would receive the same punishment as the criminals if they accepted customers without identity chits.

2. All people of the realm would be organized into a national block security system in units of ten families. Everyone had to report law violators to the authorities. A person that failed to report a crime would be executed. If one person committed a crime, all ten families of the block suffered the same penalty. However, reporting a crime was equivalent to killing an enemy officer on the battlefield and the denouncer of the deed would be rewarded in the same manner.

3. There would be twenty grades within the military system. The higher the military rank, the greater the political and economic benefits. Relatives of aristocrats without military honors were no longer eligible to register as members of the aristocracy. Senior officers were authorized to collect taxes from people within their fiefs. Military honors won on the battlefield could be used to defray civil criminal penalties, and such honors could be transferred to family members. In battle, each junior officer had to bring back the head of an enemy officer (taken by his unit) or lose his own. Any soldier who took the head of an enemy officer was to be promoted one rank and given a hectare of fertile farmland (equates to 15 *mu* or 2.5 acres of land), plus nine *mu*, an acre and a half, of land appropriate for a house, and one serf. (In ancient China, well-to-do land owners lives in the city or estates, not necessarily near the farmland.)

4. Farmers were expected to work hard on the land. Productive serfs would be freed to become citizens. Exceptional producers of grain or cloth would be exempt from annual labor levies to the realm. Failed merchants and people who did not engage in productive work would become slaves. Each family that had more than one adult male had to be split up, with each male established as head of his own household; otherwise, the taxes and labor levy duties for that family would be increased.

5. The nation's laws would apply to all people of the realm. Officials had to study and understand the laws. People who wanted to

study the laws would be taught by government officials.

6. The hereditary right to aristocratic ranks was abolished, except for the royal family. Aristocratic ranks could only be earned and maintained through military honors won on the battlefield.

7. One standardized system of official weights and measures would be used throughout the land without deviation.

* * *

The chancellor also encouraged immigration from neighboring states. He offered free farm land and housing with ten years of exemptions from taxes, plus three generations free of military and labor levy obligations. This measure increased the nation's manpower at the expense of the neighboring kingdoms.

However, at the outset, everyone, old school aristocrats as well as average people, chafed at the unusual and severe laws. On one occasion, over seven hundred people were executed at the same time for violating the new laws.

However, after three years, the population became accustomed to and liked the laws which were equally applied to everybody. The policy that forced young men to start new households enlarged the tax base and encouraged marriages and population growth. New immigrants from the neighboring states increased crop production and at the same time they freed up manpower for military duty. The granaries filled and the army grew powerful.

An additional benefit of this new regimentation was that society became law abiding and crime free. Ch'in people were usually quick to anger and arguments often ended in violence and death; now the Chancellor's edicts channeled the penchant for violence into the army.

Yang's policies encouraged the popularity of a martial mentality. People were eager for war and sought the opportunity to profit from war; men often sang and congratulated each other on hearing news of an upcoming war. However, the old guard aristocrats loathed the rules that stripped them of power, social status, and riches.

In 350 BC, Yang implemented the second phase of his reform:

1. The size of the *mu*, the unit of measurement for land, was changed from 100 paces (or yards, square) to 240 paces. The traditional feudal administrative system was abolished. People were free to own, buy and sell land.

2. The country would be divided into administrative districts, counties, and provinces, with governing officials appointed by the central government.

3. The capital of the state was to be moved from Dong-Yang to Xian-Yang.

The new laws further reduced the influence of the old school aristocrats, who were already enraged at the increased number of commoners in the ranks of nobility while the sons of the aristocratic elite were left by the wayside. Moving the capital to Xian-Yang, located near the Wei River, encouraged transportation and commerce, and expedited communications.

In 346 BC, Crown Prince Si was late for a formal ceremony, which was a major offense. It was inappropriate to punish the Crown Prince, yet the law had to be applied; so the Chancellor punished the advisor and the teacher of the Crown Prince for dereliction of duty. Gong-Tse Qian, the royal advisor, had his nose cut off; while Gong-Sun Jia, the teacher, had his face tattooed as a criminal. The punishments effectively shut off all further opposition to Yang's policies.

* * *

In 340 BC, Yang led an army to attack the Wei kingdom. Prior to the battle, Yang sent an invitation to Gong-Tse Ang, the Commander of the Wei army. The two had been good friends during Yang's tenure at the Wei court. Ang accepted the invitation with the expectation of convincing Yang to withdraw his army without bloodshed. However, Yang kept his old friend prisoner, then soundly trounced the numerically superior but leaderless Wei army.

In return for releasing Gong-Tse Ang, who was the Crown Prince of the Wei kingdom, Yang extracted all the land west of the Yellow River as ransom.

Duke Xiao gave Chancellor Yang the province of San with fifteen cities as a reward for the victory over the Wei people; henceforth, Yang became known as San Yang, meaning Yang of the San fief.

Across the border, King Hui of the Wei kingdom regretted the day that he spared the life of Yang, after his old prime minister, on his death bed, had recommended killing him. The king moved his capital from An-I eastward to Da-Liang so as to place more distance between himself and the Ch'in border.

San Yang basked in glory at his achievements and success. Zhao Liang, an acquaintance of San Yang, warned the Chancellor that his power was, after all, derived from Duke Xiao. On his path to triumph, San Yang had left too many enemies along the wayside and had created numerous adversaries. Everywhere he went, he needed scores of guards to guarantee his safety. The people feared and obeyed him, but they had no love for his severe laws that dealt out harsh punishments for even minor offenses. It would be wise for the chancellor to withdraw and retire at the prime of his power before his enemies gained control at the Ch'in court and exacted retribution. A somber San Yang pondered the matter, but he could not let go the reins of power.

Two years later, in 338 BC, Duke Xiao died and Crown Prince Si ascended to the throne. Gong-Tse Qian, who had lost his nose to San Yang's law, accused the chancellor of treason. San Yang tried to flee to the Wei kingdom, but the Wei people remembered his treachery of two years ago and they did not wish to incur the wrath of the powerful Ch'in kingdom, so they turned him away.

During his escape to the Wei kingdom, San Yang attempted to stay at an inn but was denied entry by the innkeeper for lack of a proper identity chit.

Finally, San Yang fled to his fief of San and died defending it against the new duke's army. The victorious army brought his body back to Xian-Yang, where the new duke had it drawn apart by five chariots. The people fought for a piece of his flesh to eat, to demonstrate their hatred for the deceased chancellor; as a last measure of vengeance against San Yang, his entire clan was put to the sword.

* * *

San Yang had been harsh to the point of ruthlessness in the strict execution of his policies, but he did produce results; however, he died without seeing the final outcome of his labor.

The new duke retained all the laws and policies instituted by the despised chancellor. In nineteen years, he had lifted a backwater border state into the premier nation of the land. His was the first political system in China to be governed by a centralized authority instead of feudal lords. His unification of weights and measures, the local governmental system, block security, military organization, and a multitude of other policies laid the foundation for a powerful Ch'in kingdom that ultimately unified China 117 years after his death.

His reform measures also formed the basis for the mandarin bureaucratic system that governed China for over 2,200 years. Many of his administrative policies are still in force in China and other Asian countries.

He was considered by Chinese historians to be one of the greatest visionaries and most effective prime ministers in history. They coined the phrase "San Yang Reformation" to describe his deeds and accomplishments. Without San Yang, there would not be a powerful Ch'in kingdom and consequently, we would not have China; for the name "China" originates from the Ch'in kingdom.

The anecdote regarding San Yang being denied lodging at the inn for lack of an identity chit became the popular Chinese expression, "Punished by one's own rules," which is roughly comparable to "Being hoisted by one's own petard."

In the next map, note the size and location of the Qin (Ch'in) kingdom. In 476 BC, the Jin kingdom had split into the Zhao, Han and Wei kingdoms, which marked the historical break between the Spring and Autumn Era (770–476 BC) and the Warring States Era (476–221 BC).

Chinese plain in the late Spring and Autumn period (5th century BC)

25. (Hugo Lopez — Wikimedia Commons user: Yug) China, circa 481 BC, near the end of the Spring and Autumn Era and the beginning of the Warring States Era.

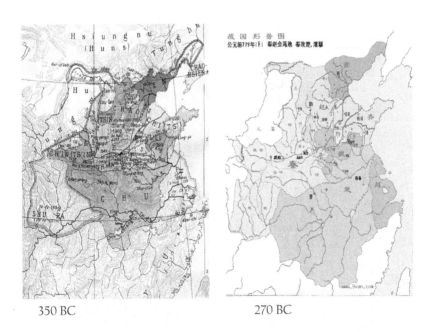

350 BC   270 BC

26. Comparative geopolitical maps of China, circa 350 BC and 270 BC. (*public domain, copyrights expired.*)

In the map on the left, the western-most triangular-shaped kingdom was the Ch'in state during the time of San Yang's administration in 350 BC. Approximately seventy years after San Yang died, the Ch'in state grew in size to dominate a third of the land as depicted in the map on the right. Another fifty years later, by 221 BC, it had completed the conquest of the other kingdoms to create the Imperial Ch'in Empire, which evolved into the China of today.

CHAPTER 7. BAI CHI, THE MOST SUCCESSFUL GENERAL IN CHINESE HISTORY

27. Bai Chi

If San Yang was the architect who designed the blueprint for the creation of a powerful kingdom, then Bai Chi was the bulldozer that cleared the land and leveled the ground for the construction of the Imperial Chinese Empire.

General Bai Chi, Duke Wu An (???–257 BC) of the Ch'in kingdom was arguably the most able and successful military commander in Chinese history if not the world. In a career that spanned more than forty years, he fought over seventy major campaigns without losing a single battle. He was a master of maneuver warfare and well known for defeating numerically superior foes. His title of

Duke Wu An translates as "The Duke who achieves peace through force of arms."

Chinese historians have estimated that during the Warring States Era over two million men perished in battles; Bai Chi was personally accountable for over half of that number. Some historians placed the figure to be closer to one and a half million.

As a commander, Bai Chi was not fixated on the capture of cities and territories; instead, he focused on the destruction of his enemy's armies. He was aggressive in combat and relentless in the pursuit of a fleeing enemy. In his preparation of the battlefield, whenever possible, he made maximum use of field fortifications and terrain to contain, weaken, and annihilate his enemies. He took into account military, geographic, political, and economic factors to analyze the upcoming battle. It was said that when he took to the field, the battle had already been won before his army marched out to meet the enemy.

* * *

28. The Warring States Era 279 BC — Ch'in (Yellow color), Han (Green color), Zhao (Light Blue color), Wei (Blue color), and Chu (Brown Color). Yeh-Wang is at the narrow connecting point in the middle of the Han kingdom.

Three of Bai Chi's signature campaigns

I. The Battle of Yi Jue (293 BC).

This was Bai Chi's first recorded major field command. The battle established Bai Chi's reputation as a military genius and his career soared until his death in 257 BC.

In 298 BC, the Qi, Wei, and Han kingdoms combined their forces to contain the Ch'in kingdom. They laid siege to the Han-Gu-Guan fortress, the gateway between the Ch'in kingdom and the central plains of eastern Central Asia. The fortress fell after three years, which forced King Zhao Xiang of the Ch'in kingdom to sue for peace in exchange for the return of all territories along the Yellow River that the Ch'in army had previously taken from the Han and Wei kingdoms. In the following year, the Han and Wei kingdoms formed an alliance to keep the Ch'in state from expanding into their territories.

In 293 BC, the kings of the Han and Wei kingdoms died; during the ensuing political instability of the two nations, King Zhao Xiang sent General Bai Chi with 115,000 men to break out of the blockade at Han-Gu-Guan.

Bai Chi faced the alliance force of over 300,000, which included a small undetermined number of troops from the Eastern Zhou kingdom. The allied armies had encamped at the Yi Jue mountain pass (the present day Long Meng — The Dragon's Gate, near Lou-Yang, He Nan Province), a strategic location between two mountains with the Yi River running through the valley.

General Gong-Sun Xi of the Wei kingdom was the nominal Commander-in-Chief of the alliance. In reality, he commanded only the Wei army, while General Bao Yuan of the Han kingdom led the Han force.

General Bao Yuan wanted the Wei army to take the lead in the upcoming battle because the Wei army was known for its discipline and ferocity. Conversely, General Gong-Sun Xi wanted the Han army to take the lead because the Wei army was the guest sent to assist the Han kingdom in the defense of the Han homeland against the Ch'in. He did not want to expend his own men before the Han army had blunted the Ch'in blade. The mutual reluctance of the two allied commanders to engage the enemy left the initiative to Bai Chi.

Bai Chi observed the enemy disposition and noted the lack of troop movements from either enemy camp. He surmised the opposing commanders' divergent views regarding the upcoming battle and made his battle plans accordingly.

The two allied forces were about equal in the number of men (about 150,000 each). They were encamped with the Han force at the fore and the Wei army several miles to the rear. Bai Chi sent a small unit with ample banners and drums to attack and distract and then pin down the Han force; meanwhile, the bulk of the Ch'in army marched around and attacked the Wei camp from the rear.

Surprised by the Ch'in attack, General Gong-Sun Xi hurried to organize his defense; at the same time, he dispatched messengers to summon reinforcements from the Han camp. However, the Han army General refused to send aid, because he too was under assault by the Ch'in army.

With no aid forthcoming from the Han army, General Gong-Sun Xi charged into battle with his personal security to rally his army. Bai Chi personally beat the drums to encourage his men into battle. General Gong-Sun was routed and taken alive. Bai Chi then pushed his men to hit the Han army from the flank, which had been deployed to face the initial Ch'in feint. The Ch'in force surprised and routed the Han army, and General Bao Yuan died with his men.

Bai Chi took the Han-Gu-Guan fortress and five additional cities from the Han kingdom. After the battle, when Gong-Sun Xi refused to surrender, Bai Chi added the Wei General's head to the trophy pile. Historians recorded 240,000 allied heads taken at Yi Jue. It was the first major campaign won by Bai Chi.

II. The Battles of Yan and Ying (279 BC)

Yan and Ying were two major cities of the Chu kingdom, the largest and arguably the most powerful nation of the land that boasted a million men under arms. With a small army, one tenth the size of his enemy, Bai Chi marched without a supply train into the Chu kingdom and captured its capital of Ying, forcing the King of Chu to flee.

By the end of the campaign, Bai Chi had conquered territory equal in size to his own kingdom and slaughtered 240,000 Chu soldiers. The Chu kingdom never recovered from the defeats at Yan and Ying, paving the way for the eventual unification of the land by the Ch'in kingdom.

* * *

In 279 BC. In 279 BC, King Zhao Xiang of the Ch'in kingdom decided to invade the Chu kingdom to the south, the largest nation in the land with over a million men under arms, but which had been weakened by internal corruption. However, King Zhao Xiang was concerned about the Zhao kingdom to the east, which had been at war with the Ch'in nation for the past two years; only a year before, Bai Chi's army took 30,000 heads during one engagement with the Zhao force. To avoid a two-front war, King Zhao Xiang brought Bai Chi along to help negotiate an armistice with the Zhao kingdom. The presence of Bai Chi prompted King Hui Wen of the Zhao kingdom to sign a peace agreement between the two nations.

Upon returning from the peace negotiation with the Zhao kingdom, Bai Chi invaded the Chu kingdom with only 100,000 men. He led the army southeastward down the bank of the Han River. Along the way, as he took each city, he destroyed bridges and burnt all shipping. The destruction of bridges and ships severed his own supply lines and demonstrated his determination for victory or death. His army foraged for food and supplies along the path of advance.

The demoralized Chu army crumbled in the face of the determined Ch'in attack, and Bai Chi quickly captured Deng, a key city in the Han River basin. As he neared Yan, a major city that was not far from the Chu capital of Ying, Bai Chi encountered a large Chu force blocking his southward advance. Bai Chi laid siege to the city, but could not break through its defenses. With a small army, deep in enemy territory and short of supplies, he needed a quick victory.

Bai Chi dammed up the Man River sixteen miles west of Yan city; then he dug a 30-mile-long canal that led to the northeastern corner of the Yan city wall. When Bai Chi broke the dam, water from the Man River flooded and broke through the Yan city's fortress wall. Several hundred thousand Chu soldiers and civilians drowned in the city, which fell to the Ch'in invaders.

Bai Chi summoned jailed criminals from the Ch'in kingdom to settle in the cities of Deng and Yan to consolidate his gains. He then got reinforcements and resupplies to resume the attack. The Ch'in army captured Ying, the capital of Chu kingdom. King Xiang Xian of Chu was forced to flee and moved his capital to the city of Cheng. The battles gave the Ch'in huge swaths of land surrounding Lake Dong-Ting and along the Yang-Tze River. For his victories in the campaign, Bai Chi was awarded the title of Duke Wu An (Duke of Martial Peace — peace through strength).

The canal dug by Bai Chi to breach the wall at Yan City became known as Bai Chi Canal; it was maintained through the ages by the local government for the irrigation of local farmlands. In 2008, the canal was registered as a historical landmark.

III. The Battle of Chang-Ping (260 BC)

The Battle of Chang-Ping was a watershed moment in Chinese history. It was the earliest recorded battle in human history where over one million men engaged in a single military campaign. It also was the greatest military disaster of ancient warfare. The victor of that struggle became the dominant power in the Far East.

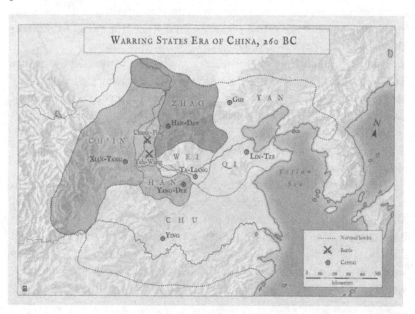

29. Chang-Ping Battle Map 1 by Maxime Plasse

Prior to the engagement, the Zhao and the Ch'in kingdoms were the premier powers. They were about equal in terms of military strength. The Zhao excelled in mounted cavalry, while the Ch'in infantry was known for its aggressiveness and ferocity. Between the two war elephants was the Tai-Xing Mountain Range. The cause and effects of this battle were one of the most debated subjects in Chinese military history.

In 262 BC, General Wang He led the Ch'in army in the invasion of the Shang Dang region of the Han kingdom. No exact figure on the size of his army is available, but a study of past Ch'in campaigns and the Zhao response force would set the Ch'in strength at between 200,000 to 300,000 men.

Wang He captured Yeh-Wang City, cutting off the Shang Dang region from the rest of the Han kingdom. Faced with its capture by the Ch'in army, the Han kingdom offered the about-to-be-captured province to the Ch'in as terms for a peace settlement. But General Feng Ting, the Han Commander of the region, had other ideas; he offered the Shang Dang territory to the neighboring Zhao kingdom instead.

The Zhao court debated General Feng's offer; accepting it would mean war against the powerful Ch'in. In the end, King Xiao Cheng of the Zhao kingdom agreed to incorporate Shang Dang into the Zhao territory, setting the stage for a military confrontation between the Ch'in and Zhao kingdoms.

General Lian Poh led 200,000 Zhao soldiers to Chang-Ping to take control of the Shang Dang region; however, by the time he reached Chang-Ping in the Tai-Xing Mountains, Shang-Dang had already fallen. General Feng Ting retreated to that city with the Ch'in army hot on his heels.

General Lian Poh sent General Zhao Chieh with 5,000 men to reconnoiter and report on the advancing Ch'in force, while Lian Poh consolidated his army with that of the local garrison force and that of Feng Ting.

At Yu Xi river valley, thirty-two kilometers west of Chang-Ping, General Zhao Chieh encountered the Ch'in vanguards led by General Shih-Ma Geng. The ensuing engagement ended poorly for the Zhao army. The Zhao general initiated the attack to catch the enemy off balance. His men were winning until a second Ch'in contingent arrived on scene. The Ch'in reinforcement surprised and routed the Zhao soldiers. General Zhao Chieh died in the melee and the leaderless Zhao force was annihilated.

Meanwhile, General Lian Poh deployed three lines of defense; the first at Kong-Chang Ridge, the second at the east bank of the Wei River, and a third along the ridges of the Tai-Xing Mountain Range. The first two lines were delaying actions to buy time for the construction of the final defense line at the Tai-Xing Mountains.

It took the Ch'in army three months before they broke through the first two lines of Zhao defenses. General Lian Poh's third defensive position was forty kilometers long, anchored atop the Tired Horse Ridge (so named because even a horse would be tired by the time it got atop the ridge). The general established ten garrisons and had his men dig cisterns. The cisterns order perplexed the men but it proved prophetic when the Ch'in army cut off access to the Wei River. The Zhao army settled atop their final defensive line and easily beat back the Ch'in attackers.

Wang He encamped his army on the valley floor facing the Zhao defenses, daring the Zhao general to attack. General Lian Poh refused to be goaded into battle. He forbade his men to attack the enemy. The Ch'in army had a hundred-mile-long supply line over water and rugged terrain. He intended to wait until the Ch'in army got tired and withdrew, when they would be vulnerable to attack from the mobile Zhao cavalry. The lack of battlefield victories infuriated the King of Zhao, but Lian Poh refused to go on the offensive, even when commanded to do so by his king. Lian Poh practiced the military axiom — *A commander in the field need not obey every order from the king.*

To break out of the impasse at Chang-Ping, Fan Sui, the Prime Minister of the Ch'in kingdom, sent spies to the Zhao court and bribed courtiers to whisper rumors into the King Xiao Cheng's ears. "Duke Ma Fu was the best general of the Zhao Kingdom; but his son Zhao Gua is supposedly even better than his father. Zhao Gua is the person that the Ch'in people fear on the battlefield. Lian Poh is old and feeble; he already lost several battles and cost us more than 30,000 men. Faced with continued Ch'in pressure, Lian Poh might falter and surrender to the enemy."

The rumors dovetailed with news from the front. The initial battle losses were major blows to the morale of the Zhao kingdom. The king fell for the ruse and replaced General Lian Poh with General Zhao Gua. Zhao Gua was the son of the famous General Zhao Ser, the Duke Ma Fu, who had decimated the Ch'in army that had previously invaded the Zhao kingdom through those same mountains.

General Zhao Gua had no field experience. His military knowledge was acquired through books; his own mother opposed his appointment as the Zhao army commander. She even petitioned the king to absolve her clan of blame in the event of a failure by her son.

When news of Zhao Gua's replacement of Lian Poh reached the Ch'in capital of Xian-Yang, the King of Ch'in dispatched Bai Chi to be the senior commander over General Wang He and directed, on pain of death, the change of command be kept secret.

At Chang-Ping, Bai Chi assumed command of the Ch'in army and surveyed the terrain. He abandoned the aggressive infantry attacks traditionally favored by the Ch'in force; instead, he fortified the southern and western rims of the valley by the Wei River, then waited for the enemy to come to him.

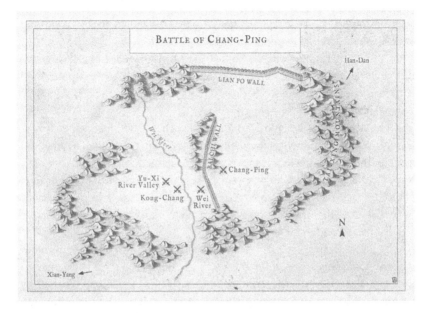

30. Chang-Ping Battle Map 2 by Maxime Plasse

Zhao Gua led 200,000 reinforcements to join Lian Poh's force at Chang-Ping and took over the command of the Zhao army. Lian Poh relinquished his command, then left for Han-Dan. The new Zhao commander immediately replaced Lien's Poh's senior commanders with his own officers; then summoned together all the garrison forces. When he announced his decision to go on the offensive, eight senior officers objected to the change in strategy; the enraged Zhao Gua personally butchered the eight generals for insubordination and cowardice.

He sent a messenger to the Ch'in encampment to deliver a challenge to battle. Bai Chi used Wang He's name in accepting the challenge. On his return to the Zhao camp, the messenger reported that the Ch'in army was striking camp.

Meanwhile, Bai Chi made his preparations and issued battle orders. He sent Generals Wang Ben and Wang Ling with 10,000 men each to block the Zhao army's main line of advance. They were to engage, then retreat when pressed by the enemy. Generals Shih-Ma Tsou and Shih-Ma Geng took 15,000 men each to circle behind the advancing Zhao army and cut its supply lines. General Hu Sang would lie in ambush with 20,000 men; he was to allow the main Zhao assault force to march past before assaulting the Zhao reserve force at the base camp. He would sever the communication lines between the advancing Zhao force and its base camp. Generals Meng Aou and Wang Jien were to deploy with 5,000 light cavalry each as a ready reaction force. Generals Bai Chi and Wang He remained at the base camp with the main force to monitor and direct the battle.

General Zhao Gua ordered half of his army to guard the base camp and cover the rear while being prepared to follow-up with supplies and reinforcements when ordered to do so. He then marshaled the other 200,000 men to seek battle with the enemy.

Commanders Fu Bao and Wang Zong led the 20,000 men vanguards in search for the enemy, with the main force following behind. They had no trouble finding the Ch'in advance force and charged into them before they could deploy for battle. Caught by surprise, the Ch'in force fell back. When Zhao Gua received the report of the victory, he ordered a full-scale pursuit. General Feng Ting, the Han army commander, cautioned against a trap — which Zhao Gua ignored.

The Zhao advance force pursued the fleeing enemy into the late afternoon, with the Zhao Gua's army following closely behind; then the Zhao vanguard halted at the mouth of the valley when they found their way blocked by the fortified battlements of the Ch'in encampment. Unable to continue the attack, the two officers withdrew out of missile range, then sorted the men into their respective units while they waited for the main body to link up.

The Zhao advance force lacked siege equipment, so General Zhao Gua ordered signalers to beat the gongs. It was the command for the men to pull back and regroup. He wanted time to plan and organize a proper assault on the enemy fortification. However, just as the Zhao soldiers responded to the withdrawal signals, the Ch'in army sprang their trap.

While the sounds of Zhao signal gongs were still echoing off the canyon walls, the Ch'in army atop the fortification countered with a thundering drum roll. At the end of the drum beats, scores of large black and gold pennants appeared on the battlement, each with the bold white word 'Bai' inscribed in its center. Before its meaning sank in, General Bai Chi stepped onto the rampart.

Duke Wu An lifted his right hand and the second roll of drums sounded from the Ch'in palisades, this time at a higher tone and with a faster beat. The second drum signal was relayed throughout the mountains in the canyon. As the drums thumped, the gates of the Ch'in encampment swung wide. Accompanied by a great roar that reverberated in the mountain valley, Ch'in soldiers poured out to attack the withdrawing Zhao force. At the same time, ambushers emerged from their hidden positions in the mountainsides and assaulted the Zhao flanks.

The sudden appearance of Duke Wu An shocked Zhao Gua. The Zhao army froze while the enemy advanced on their rear and sides. The Zhao force was in disarray; the men closest to the enemy were the original vanguards, but they were also the first to obey the withdrawal command and had already started marching toward the rear, and thus were unprepared to receive an enemy assault. Meanwhile, the men in the center and rear of the Zhao column still faced the enemy, but they were blocked by their comrades who were in the process of withdrawing from the front. The organized redeployment quickly degenerated into a chaotic mess.

Soldiers closest to the advancing assault tried to flee from the fury of the enemy's charge, further deteriorating the situation. Men fell, then got trampled by their comrades; war chariots overturned and officers shouted confusing and conflicting orders, none of which could be heard over the din of the drums and war cries, much less be obeyed. In the tidal wave of chaotic masses, General Zhao Gua tried to order the men closest to the enemy to turn around again and form a rearguard; but troop commanders couldn't hear his commands. He had lost control of the army.

Then, riders arrived with alarming news from the rear of the column; in the direction of the Zhao base camp, enemy cavalry had blocked their routes of retreat. General Zhao Gua tried to make order out of the disorganized situation. He commanded the men to take up defensive positions in place and dispatched messengers for supplies and reinforcements. The army was to fight and hold its position until the reserve force came up to relieve it. They prayed that some of the messengers would get through to ask for help.

Again, General Feng Ting objected to his commander's order; General Feng urged his commander to resume the offensive while the army still had the strength and the will to fight. General Feng argued that they had a numerical advantage over the enemy in front of them and could still win the battle if they would only concentrate the men and smash ahead into the enemy's attack. He called this the 'Snatch Life Out of the Death Trap' strategy. Since the enemy expected the Zhao army to retreat from the surprise ambushes, the army should turn the surprise back against the ambushers to break out of the trap. If nothing else, the army should continue fighting its way back to the base camp, since the confined terrain in the valley could not possibly support the logistical needs of 200,000 men.

General Zhao Gua rejected the idea because General Feng Ting had been the commander of the Han army that had been defeated by the enemy earlier in the campaign. General Zhao Gua wanted time to reorganize his forces into orderly units that could properly execute his battle plans. He had the men build defensive positions in place and prepared to fend off enemy assaults, while he planned a breakout from the valley.

Meanwhile, at Xian-Yang, the capital of the Ch'in kingdom, the king received news of the successful entrapment of the Zhao army. King Zhao Xiang mobilized every able-bodied male age fifteen or older in the eastern provinces and personally led them to reinforce the front. Bai Chi deployed the new arrivals to strengthen the blockade and encirclement of Zhao Gua's position.

The expected Ch'in assault against the entrapped Zhao army never took place; instead, the Ch'in soldiers strengthened their blockades while cutting the Zhao army's supply routes and establishing roadblocks at all passes through the mountainous terrain. They left the Zhao army to rot in their makeshift shelters. The 200,000 men were confined within a small mountain valley, and they suffered from horrendous deprivation, thirst, hunger and cold. While Zhao soldiers huddled in their makeshift encampment, Ch'in soldiers taunted their enemies with loud and raucous feasts on captured Zhao supplies.

General Zhao Gua organized his force into four units; each took turns assaulting the Ch'in barricades. Zhao assaults met hails of bolts and arrows from well-fortified positions, followed by counterattacks from members of the dreaded 'Bare Head Brigade,' Ch'in berserker warriors who fought with neither helmet nor armor; some even fought bare-chested.

Time and again Zhao soldiers charged; each and every time they were contained and beaten back into their confined cauldron. The situation in the Zhao camp became worse than desperate near the last days of the entrapment. Thirsty men fought each other for a swallow of dirty dew water. All the horses had been butchered for food, eliminating the most effective fighting force of the Zhao army. At the end, men were gnawing on horses' hoofs and leather coverings of their shields. There were even reports of cannibalism. With no hope of relief, on the forty-sixth day of the encirclement, General Zhao Gua summoned the officers and ordered one all-out breakout. Before launching the final attack, the general removed his armor and left word that he was to be buried with a white cloth covering his face, for he was too ashamed to meet his father in the afterlife.

Zhao soldiers trudged out tired and hungry to face their enemies. Zhao Gua personally led 5,000 elite forces in the van of the attack. Again, the Ch'in crossbowmen held their ground. Zhao Gua and his command staff died in a shower of missiles. General Feng Ting committed suicide by cutting his own throat.

Bai Chi ordered his men to wave his pennant and called for the Zhao soldiers to surrender. In no time, the battlefield was covered with Zhao soldiers prostrated in submission to the Ch'in victors. Bai Chi chopped off Zhao Gua's head, then sent it to the Zhao base camp at Chang-Ping, demanding its surrender. Leaderless, the 200,000 garrison force gave up without a fight.

Bai Chi separated the prisoners into ten encampments and announced that the Ch'in army would absorb the strong and able captives into its ranks. Those not chosen would be sent home to the Zhao kingdom after the armistice. He ordered food and wine for the prisoners. Zhao soldiers cheered and cried in relief; they thanked the gods for their reprieve. That night, Ch'in soldiers entered the prison camps with white cloths over their heads. They butchered every person without a white head cover. Tired, and satiated with food and wine, most of the victims died in their sleep; those able to escape from the encampment encountered Meng Aou's and Wang Jian's cavalrymen, who immediately dispatched the prisoners to share the fate of their comrades.

In one night, Bai Chi's army turned 400,000 men into ghosts. Added to the losses suffered by Feng Tien and Lian Poh earlier in the campaign, the Zhao kingdom lost 450,000 men at Chang-Ping. Wei River's water turned red from blood, and the river became known as Red Water.

Bai Chi spared 240 youths among the prisoners, so that they could go home and spread the news of the great Ch'in victory and strike fear into the hearts of the enemies.

The royal court at Han-Dan bathed in fear and tears; everyone dreaded the impending arrival of the Ch'in army at the city gates. Mournful cries filled the city as news of the Chang-Ping massacres spread, adding to the air of despair. Not one household in the entire Zhao kingdom escaped without losing a close family member or relative at Chang-Ping. The Zhao King sent Su Dai, a persuasive courtier, with a large sum of gold and jewelry to Xian-Yang to seek a peaceful resolution.

At Xian-Yang, Su Dai gained an audience with Fan Sui, the Ch'in Prime Minister, and convinced him that it would be politically expedient to accept the Zhao kingdom's offer of six cities in exchange for a negotiated peace treaty. This way the prime minister would have the honor of gaining territory without the use of force, while preventing his political rival, Duke Wu An, from becoming the king's favorite at the Ch'in Court.

Fan Sui advised the Ch'in King that the army had been in the field too long. With the victory at Chang-Ping, an opportunity existed to diplomatically gain land in exchange for withdrawing the army. The kingdom stood to gain territory without a fight while giving the army and the national economy a chance to recover from the prolonged warfare. The king consented to his prime minister's suggestion and ordered a recall of Bai Chi's army.

Bai Chi had been preparing to march on Han-Dan when he received the recall order. It was a very irate Duke Wu An who returned to Xian-Yang. He argued that, in the wake of the Chang-Ping disaster, Han-Dan would have fallen with a slight military demonstration in that direction. The king realized the missed opportunity and attempted to rectify the mistake. However, Bai Chi petulantly refused the offer to command the new expedition, claiming he had taken ill and was unable to take to the field. Instead, General Wang Ling led 100,000 men to attack Han-Dan. By then, the Zhao kingdom had recovered from the disaster and General Lian Poh led an energetic and successful defense of the Zhao capital, thus, avoiding a complete and total defeat to the Ch'in army.

The Chang-Ping massacre was a near mortal blow to the Zhao kingdom. It had lost ten percent of its population in one fell swoop. That damage is increased when assessed in terms of the able-bodied male population. Prior to the conflict, the Zhao kingdom was an effective obstacle between the Ch'in kingdom and the central plains of eastern Asia; afterward, Zhao became a shell of its former self and no longer posed a significant obstacle to Ch'in's grand design for conquest.

In the final analysis, the Ch'in army could have taken Han-Dan and the Zhao kingdom in the immediate aftermath of the Chang-Ping disaster. The truce Su Dai arranged gave the Zhao people time to recover psychologically and organize its defenses against the Ch'in army. The massacre may have struck fear into many people, but it also steeled the will of the Zhao citizenry to fight to the end; not to mention the desire to seek revenge for the murder of their loved ones. Finally, it prompted other kingdoms of the land to band together against the might of the Ch'in army.

Nevertheless, within thirty-two years (228 BC), King Zheng, the great grandson of King Zhao Xiang, marched his troops into Han-Dan. Seven years after that, King Zheng completed the unification of China and made himself "Ch'in Shi Huang Di — the First Emperor." Ironically, Zheng was born in Han-Dan in 259 BC, one year after the Chang-Ping massacre; his father, Prince Yi Ren, a grandson of King Zhao Xiang, had been a political exchange-hostage in the Zhao Court.

The importance of the Chang-Ping battle cannot be overstated. Had the Zhao army prevailed in that battle, the Ch'in kingdom would have been bottled up in western Asia; thus "China," the heir of the "Ch'in" kingdom, would not have come into existence.

Subsequent to the peace settlement, the Zhao kingdom reneged on ceding the six cities. King Zhao Xiang summoned Bai Chi to renew the attack on Han-Dan. Again, the Duke Wu An demurred; he felt the opportunity for the conquest of Zhao had passed. He believed the Zhao people had had time to bury their sorrow and would be seeking revenge, and the other kingdoms would rally to aid Zhao, to contain the Ch'in expansion.

The persistent King Zhao Xiang sent General Wang Ling to command the expedition. When Wang Ling suffered defeat with heavy casualties, the king felt he needed Bai Chi. He sent the prime minister to persuade Duke Wu An to accept the appointment. Bai Chi recalled Fan Sui's treachery of the previous year, and claiming illness, declined to take to the field. The king personally visited Bai Chi to discuss the issue. The general told the king, "By accepting the command of the army, I could suffer defeat and still live; however, I could die for refusing the offer of the command. Please do not give the order to have me command the army." The king relented and selected Wang He to replace Wang Ling.

For nine months, Wang He laid siege to Han-Dan but failed to breach that city's walls. Meanwhile, the kingdoms of Chu and Wei sent 200,000 men to aid the Zhao kingdom. The allied forces soundly trounced Wang He's army.

On hearing the news of the defeat at Han-Dan, Bai Chi was said to have sneered, "See what happens when you don't heed my counsel?" The Duke's enemies passed the remark to the prime minister's ears, then into that of the king. The irate king ordered Bai Chi to go forth and assume command of the army. Duke Wu An again claimed illness and defied the king's order.

For that final insubordination, the king stripped Bai Chi of his position, demoted him to the rank of a common soldier, and exiled him to the western border town of Ying Mi. Bai Chi delayed his departure from Xian-Yang, claiming lingering illness. After three months of dawdling, at the urging of the prime minister, the king sent a courtier with an escort of royal guardsmen to evict Bai Chi from the city.

Fan Sui told the king that on receipt of the eviction order, Bai Chi had grumbled at his unjust treatment. At Du Yew, a city ten li's west of the Xian-Yang, Bai Chi received one final royal edict — the king had sent his personal sword to the exiled, aged, common soldier. Holding the royal sword in his hand, Bai Chi lifted his head toward Heaven and asked the Gods, "What sin have I committed to merit this predicament?" After a slight pause, he gave a reply to his own question. "I deserve to die, for at Chang-Ping, I lied to and massacred 400,000 Zhao prisoners; for that alone, I deserve to die." With those final words, he slit his own throat with the king's sword.

On hearing the news of his death, his former foes in the other kingdoms celebrated with glee and toasted his demise. Chang-Ping was the apex of Bai Chi's military career, on the cusp of reaching an even higher plateau with the conquest of the once mighty Zhao kingdom; however, court intrigue deprived him of that glory and caused his ultimate downfall.

For his atrocities at Chang-Ping, Chinese historians nicknamed Bai Chi "The Butcher." It should be pointed out that the Zhao kingdom had been the doorstop that kept the Ch'in nation out of the central plains of Eastern Asia. The Zhao kingdom had lost one tenth of its population at Chang-Ping and thus could no longer hold back the Ch'in onslaught. Thirty-nine years after Chang-Ping, the Ch'in state vanquished the other kingdoms and completed the unification of China.

Counting the reinforcements brought by King Zhao Xiang to Chang-Ping, the Ch'in kingdom had committed over half a million men to that campaign. According to Bai Chi, in spite of the victory, the Ch'in army had suffered over fifty percent casualties in the campaign.

If the Zhao kingdom had defeated the Ch'in army at Chang-Ping, the modern geopolitical landscape of eastern Asia would have been drastically altered. A defeat at Chang-Ping would have left the Ch'in state vulnerable to invasion by the powerful Chu kingdom to the south. With its greater land mass and larger population, the Chu kingdom stood a good chance to unify the land. In any case, China would not have come into being as a great imperial empire and there would have been no Silk Road for trading with the west. Finally, the Warring States Era (476–221 BC) which had ended with the unification of the land would have continued on. Consequently, in modern times, we might have found a multitude of nation states competing for supremacy in that distant land we now know as China.

Had Bai Chi been allowed to follow up on his victory at Chang-Ping and complete the conquest of the Zhao kingdom, the other nations in the vicinity might have given up out of fear. It would have accelerated the unification of China by forty years. He was without a doubt the greatest military commander of Chinese history, if not the world.

31. Bai Chi Rou — Flesh of Bai Chi

At Gao-Ping, Shanxi Province, a famous dish is served — *Bai Chi Rou* (Flesh of Bai Chi). The Zhao people created the culinary item to vent their anger against Bai Chi for massacring 400,000 Zhao prisoners. They grilled tofu over the stove and ate it with a mixture of ginger, garlic and tofu paste sauce. Eating *Bai Chi Rou* was akin to eating the flesh of Bai Chi.

In contrast, the Ch'in people sympathized with his innocence and revered Bai Chi for his accomplishments. They made sacrificial offerings to him and voluntarily built a mausoleum in his honor at Xian-Yang. Thirty-five years after his death, Zheng, the great-grandson of King Zhao Xiang and the First Emperor of China, rehabilitated Bai Chi posthumously and restored his family title and estate in the city of Tai-Yuan, in the present day Shanxi Province.

CHAPTER 8. GAN LUO, THE DIPLOMATIC GENIUS

In 235 BC, Prime Minister Lu Bu-Wei of the Ch'in kingdom wanted to dispatch Zhang Tang to the Yan kingdom to negotiate an alliance against the Zhao nation. Yan sits east of the Zhao while the Ch'in is west of that nation. Lu wants to coordinate a joint attack against the Zhao. However, Zhang was reluctant to accept the mission because he had previously commanded an army that invaded the Zhao; he was concerned that Zhao people might kill him when he travels through the Zhao territory to the Yan kingdom.

Gan Luo, an advisor to Lu Bu-Wei, was the grandson of the famous former Prime Minister Gan Mao of the Ch'in kingdom. Gan Luo visited Zhang to change his mind.

"Master Zhang, need I remind you of the reason that General Bai Chi, the best general in history, was forced to commit suicide?" Zhang nodded but did not reply. "He refused then Prime Minister Fan Sui's request to lead an army against the Zhao people. As a result, the king ordered Bai Chi to commit suicide.

"Now, you and I both know that Prime Minister Lu is infinitely more powerful than Fan Sui ever was." The argument convinced Zhang, however unwilling, to accept the assignment to the Yan kingdom. Gan noted Zhang's hesitation. "Now, don't worry, I will make a trip to Han-Dan to pave the way for you."

Gan volunteered for a diplomatic mission to Han-Dan, capital of the Zhao kingdom. King You Miao was surprised at the youthful ambassador, but his surprise ended when Gan stated the purpose of his visit. "Your Majesty, you are aware that Prince Dan of the Yan nation has arrived at Xian-Yang to serve as exchange hostage, and in return, my king will be sending Zhang Tang to serve as a minister of the Yan court?"

"Yes, I know Dan is at Xian-Yang and Zhang will be traveling to Ji."

"But, are you not concerned? The purpose of his mission is to arrange a coordinated attack against your kingdom."

The king frowned, "That's what I heard; and why are you telling me this?"

"The reason my kingdom wants to war on you is to capture the He-Jian territories and the five cities there.

"Now, if you agree to cede the five cities and He-Jian territories to us, I can persuade my king to sever the alliance with Yan. That will give you a free hand to invade the Yan, and we will not interfere or attack you from the west. This way you trade five cities in the west for a whole lot more in the east."

King You Miao liked the idea. He gave Gan Luo a map that marked out the He-Jian region and its five cities which were to be ceded to the Ch'in kingdom. In addition, Gan received 100 *taels* of gold and a set of precious white jade as gifts from the king.

As promised, the Ch'in severed the alliance with the Yan kingdom, and the Zhao army attacked and took 30 cities from the Yan state. The King of Zhao then made a gift of eleven of the captured cities to the Ch'in nation for not attacking the Zhao while their army was engaged with the Yan people.

Without sending out an army, Gan Luo got all the He-Jian territories, its five cities and eleven Yan cities for the Ch'in kingdom. For his ingenious diplomatic coup, Gan Luo was promoted to be a minister of the Ch'in court and received all the fiefs that used to belong to his grandfather.

At the time, Gan Luo the genius diplomat was only twelve years old.

CHAPTER 9. KONG MING, THE CHINESE LEONARDO DA VINCI

32. Kong Ming

Kong Ming (AD 181–234), also known as Zhu-Ge Liang, was considered by many Chinese as the most brilliant man in history. He was an accomplished scholar, statesman, military strategist, administrator, inventor, astrologer, and meteorologist.

Kong Ming was the ideal Chinese hero. His patron, Liu Bei, was a refugee aristocrat who made three personal visits to Kong Ming's home to seek his assistance. Kong Ming repaid Liu Bei's trust with 28 years of loyal service. With Kong Ming's help, Liu Bei rose from an insignificant nobleman to become a king.

At the onset of the Battle of Red Cliff, Kong Ming persuaded the neighboring Wu kingdom to join in the fight against Cao Cao, leader of the Wei kingdom. With an army of a mere 30,000 men, the alliance decimated an enemy force of 800,000. The prestige and the territory gained from that battle enabled Liu Bei to establish his Su kingdom.

As an innovator, Kong Ming invented mechanical horses and oxen to transport military supplies to the front line. Unfortunately, no records or blueprints of these devices survived his passing. He invented the Kong Ming Lantern, known in the West as the Chinese lantern that flies like a kite. Kong Ming developed it to transmit messages to summon reinforcements for his army.

He also modified the crossbow into a multiple firing ballista system to bolster the firepower of his small army.

However, Kong Ming was most famous for his military stratagem and the use of human psychology. In AD 225, Kong Ming led his army against a regional rebellion led by a man named Meng Huo. Kong Ming captured the rebel leader seven times and released him each time. After the seventh release, Meng Huo surrendered of his own free will and swore eternal allegiance to the Su kingdom.

In return for the promise of allegiance from Meng Huo, Kong Ming withdrew his army and left Meng Huo's people to choose their own leaders and govern themselves. The policy allowed the Su kingdom to rule Meng Huo's territory in peace without the expenditure of men or resources while gaining control of a large territory rich in resources and manpower.

Kong Ming's expedition against Meng Huo provides a contrast to the American expedition against Geronimo, the Apache Indian chief who was pursued by General Cook in the American Southwest. In Meng Huo's case, at the end of the campaign, Kong Ming left Meng Huo as an obedient vassal, providing men and supplies to the Su kingdom, while in the case of Geronimo, he spent most of his post-war years as a prisoner, costing the US government men and resources to maintain control over the Indian Territory.

One of the most often recounted folktales among Chinese people involves the "Empty City Strategy." Kong Ming was the hero of said tactical ploy. Circa AD 227, Ma Su, a general under Kong Ming's command, disregarded Kong Ming's instructions and lost a crucial battle, which left Kong Ming vulnerable at Xi Cheng with 2,500 men against an enemy force of 150,000 led by Shi-Ma Yi of the Wei kingdom.

With no time to escape, Kong Ming removed all the banners and hid his troops from sight. He sent soldiers disguised in civilian clothing to water and sweep the parade grounds around the city's gates. Shi-Ma Yi's vanguards found the city undefended with all four gates wide open. They halted and reported the information to their superiors.

Shi-Ma Yi arrived at the city gate and saw Kong Ming seated atop the battlement flanked by two pages as he played music on a 'glen,' a long thirteen-fretted instrument.

Shi-Ma Yi knew Kong Ming's reputation as a strategist not given to rash or risky ventures. The open city gates appeared to be an invitation to attack. Shi-Ma Yi hesitated and allowed discretion to overcome valor. He withdrew, thus allowing Kong Ming and his men to escape. Henceforth, the phrase 'Empty City Strategy' became synonymous with the 'Great Bluff.'

33. Kong Ming at the 'Bluff'

In 234 BC, the two opponents once again faced off against each other. This time, Kong Ming was the invader. Wary of Kong Ming's tactical genius, Shi-Ma Yi fought a cautious defensive campaign. He refused an all-out decisive engagement with the crafty opponent.

He knew Kong Ming had a long logistical tail and needed a quick decisive battle; Shi-Ma Yi wisely declined to accommodate. Kong Ming sent Shi-Ma Yi a set of a woman's garments to provoke the Wei general, who ignored the insult.

After three months of this standoff, Kong Ming died of illness and his army withdrew from the field. That was when Shi-Ma Yi gave chase to his enemy. Suddenly, the retreating Su army turned around and attacked their pursuers. Shi-Ma Yi thought Kong Ming had faked his death to spring another trap, so he ordered an immediate retreat; thus he allowed the Su army to once again elude a defeat by Shi-Ma Yi.

Shi-ma Yi had fallen for yet another of Kong Ming's strategies. The Su counterattack had been another bluff to hold off the pursuing Wei army.

Kong Ming had planned the counterattack maneuver and reached out from his grave and, for one last time, bested his enemy.

To this date, numerous temples and statues of Kong Ming dot the landscape of China and Taiwan, honoring the loyal strategist who repeatedly outsmarted his enemies. It should be noted that on his deathbed, Liu Bei offered the throne of the Su kingdom to Kong Ming, but Kong Ming declined.

Historical note:

Kong Ming's "Great Bluff" against Shi-ma Yi at Xi Cheng was a fable born out of the "Romance of the Three Kingdoms" with no historical basis. However, the tale encapsulates so well the renowned genius of Kong Ming that it reveals a truth even through fiction.

CHAPTER 10. WU QI, THE FLAWED PERFECT GENERAL

Wu Qi

吴起贪将，杀妻自信，散金求官，母死不归，然在魏，秦人不敢东向，在楚则三晋不敢南谋。

——**曹操**

Wu Qi murdered his wife for a command, paid a bribe to acquire rank, and refused to grieve for his deceased mother; yet when he was at Wei kingdom, the Ch'in people dared not attack eastward, and when he was at Chu kingdom, the Three Jin states were afraid to move south.

Commentary on General Wu Qi, by Cao Cao (AD 155–220), Prime Minister of Eastern Han Dynasty

Most students of military history consider Sun Tzu, author of *The Art of War*, as the premier military theoretician of ancient China. It is a claim that many Chinese military historians would dispute. Wu Qi (440–381 BC), a less renowned contemporary of Sun Tzu, was viewed by many Chinese to be a superior military leader, and he had the numbers to back them up. He even has a 2,400-year-old city, Wu-Cheng (Wu city), named after him.

Wu Qi's many character flaws did not fit the traditional Chinese image (or anyone else's) of an iconic hero. He was vain, avaricious, lecherous, ambitious, and unlucky. Therefore, he was not well regarded by Confucian scholars who dominated China's literary elite, which resulted in a paucity of written material on him and ultimately contributed to the lack of knowledge about him, both in China and abroad.

However, his personal failings should not detract from his undisputed status as an exceptional military leader.

Wu Qi lived during the beginning of the Warring States Era (476–221 BC). He grew up in the small kingdom of Way (in Central-Eastern China) from humble beginnings and rose to become one of the greatest military leaders of all times.

As a young man, Wu Qi did not demonstrate any special talent worthy of notice. He preferred swordplay over books and associated with local ruffians. His mother despaired at the young man's misbehavior and often chastised Wu Qi for his misdeeds.

One day, after another round of sharp rebukes from his mother, Wu Qi bit the bicep of his own arm and used the blood for an oath. "I am leaving and shall not return until I have made a name for myself, and will come home in a carriage with riches and honor."

Surprised by the unexpected angry outburst, his mother pleaded for Wu Qi to stay home; but no words from his mother could dissuade Wu Qi from going on his way.

He traveled east to the Lu kingdom, the homeland of the renowned philosopher Confucius, and entered the school of Tseng Sen, a learned scholar, and a son of Tseng Tsan, who was a renowned disciple of Confucius.

Wu Qi studied Confucian classics and philosophy with the aim of becoming a courtier. Trained in the humanities and literary classics, Confucian scholars were always in high demand at royal courts. They were prized for their knowledge, diplomatic skills, and above all else, loyalty. Confucius himself had served as a courtier for the Lord of the Lu state.

Wu Chi's diligent hard work and talent soon paid off in unexpected dividends. Tien Ghu, a minister of the neighboring Qi kingdom, happened to visit Tseng Sen's school. Wu Qi's knowledge and demeanor quickly impressed the visitor. At the end of the visit, Minister Tien gave one of his daughters to Wu Qi to be his wife, to cement a relationship that would be continued in the future — when Wu Qi had completed his studies with Tseng Sen.

After Minister Tien departed, the teacher summoned Wu Qi to learn more about the student's family background. However, the school master's congenial demeanor turned to rage when he learned Wu Qi had sworn a blood oath to his mother, a very disrespectful treatment of one's mother that violated the basic Confucian tenet of obedience and respect to authorities, which encompassed filial loyalty to the parents.

Not long afterward, a messenger brought word that Wu Qi's mother had passed away. On hearing the news of his mother's death, Wu Qi lifted his head and howled three tearful cries to heaven, then wiped dry his tears and resumed his studies.

When Tseng Sen heard of the incident, he was incensed that Wu Qi had so little regard for his mother's passing and evicted Wu Qi from the school.

Frustrated, Wu Qi abandoned the study of literary classics to pursue the martial arts.

Three years later, He returned to the Lu kingdom and visited Gon Ei Hsiu, the prime minister. Gon remembered Wu Qi as an exceptional student in Tseng Sen's school and a son-in-law of a minister in the powerful Qi kingdom to the north.

Wu Qi impressed the prime minister with his knowledge of military doctrines and leadership techniques. Gon Ei Hsiu persuaded Duke Mu, ruler of the Lu state, to appoint Wu Qi as a minister of the Court.

The new courtier wasted no time in acquiring several concubines as befitting a person of his rank and social status.

Just as Wu Qi settled down into his new found riches, trouble brewed in the north. In the neighboring Qi nation, Tien He, the prime minister, usurped the throne of the kingdom. He feared that Duke Mu of the Lu kingdom, who was related by marriage to the deposed King of Qi, would contest the coup d'état in the Qi nation. The new ruler of Qi sent an army to preempt a possible Lu attempt to restore the old king to his throne.

Duke Mu wanted Wu Qi to drive off the invaders but hesitated because Wu Qi was related by marriage to the new King of the Qi nation. The duke discussed his concerns regarding Wu Qi with his prime minister, who related the duke's reservations to Wu Qi.

The following day, Wu Qi visited the court and presented the severed head of his wife to the duke as a testament of loyalty. The maneuver horrified the duke, who waved off the trophy but nevertheless gave Wu Qi the command of the army.

Wu Qi led his army north to face the Qi invaders. His leadership style surprised and endeared him to his men. Instead of riding in the command chariot, he walked beside his troops. At camp, he ate with the average soldiers and slept on the ground like his men. On the march, he carried his own rations and equipment. With those simple deeds, General Wu Qi gained the loyalty and the respect of his army. The men under his command were ready to face the devil if the general deemed it so.

Spies from the Qi army reported information regarding Wu Qi and his army to Tien He, Lord and Commander of the Qi army. Tien He sneered at Wu Qi's leadership style. "Although he is a son-in-law of my clan, the man indulges too much in pretty women and lacks military experience. The Lu army shall be defeated."

Wu Qi halted his army a short distance from the Qi invaders and kept his men in camp. He made no move to provoke a battle.

Surprised at the inactivity of the Lu army, Tien He sent spies to scout out the Lu encampment. They saw Wu Qi seated on the ground sharing porridge with a group of common soldiers.

After receiving the report, Tien He smirked, "Familiarity breeds contempt. A general should demonstrate his elite status and superiority to the men to command their respect, so they will be obedient and fight hard for him. Wu Qi obviously does not understand the basic tenets of command leadership. I am not worried about the outcome of the coming battle."

He sent General Chang Ynew to the Lu encampment, under the pretext of peace negotiations with Wu Qi to spy on the enemy's preparedness and intentions.

Wu Qi hid his best troops from view while parading older, weaker men in the encampment. He treated the Qi general with extreme courtesy. Chang Ynew felt gratified and honored with his reception and annotated his observations before returning to his base camp.

Unbeknownst to Chang Ynew, Wu Qi sent three columns of troops to trail him back to his encampment. Chang Ynew's report convinced the Qi commander that the Lu army was weak, with no stomach for fighting. When the Lu army attacked the Qi encampment, it was a complete surprise.

The Lu army returned in triumph to Chu Fu, the capital of the Lu kingdom, and the elated Duke Mu rewarded Wu Qi with a promotion to Minister of the Senior Rank.

Meanwhile, at Lin Tse, the capital of the Qi kingdom, Tien He lamented, "Wu Qi is obviously a general that is an equal to Sun Tzu. As long as that man serves the Lu kingdom, we are at risk. I want someone to go and negotiate terms with him."

Chang Ynew volunteered for the task, to atone for his earlier blunder. He arrived at Wu Chi's residence in Chu Fu disguised as a merchant. He brought two beautiful women and a thousand taels of gold for Wu Qi, who accepted the gifts and promised not to invade the Qi if they did not attack the Lu kingdom.

Upon leaving the city, Chang Ynew intentionally leaked news of the bribery. Rumors of a pact between General Wu Qi and the ruler of the northern rival Qi state quickly reached the Lu court. The already suspicious Duke Mu immediately executed Gon for sponsoring Wu Qi into the Lu Court, then sent men to arrest Wu Qi. The fugitive general abandoned his new found riches and fled to An-Ee, capital of the Wei kingdom.

He found refuge with Dee Heng, an official in the Wei Royal Court. Dee knew Lord Wen of Wei needed a good general to guard the West River territories (the land west of the Yellow River), a key region that bordered the powerful Ch'in kingdom; Dee presented Wu to Lord Wen, who appointed Wu Qi as the Governor of the West River Region.

Wu Qi took command of his new post and treated his men as he had in the Lu kingdom. To fortify the frontier, he built a city that still carries his name, Wu-Cheng (The City of Wu, or Wu's City).

When Duke Hui, ruler of the Ch'in kingdom, died, Wu Qi took advantage of the political instability in that kingdom and captured five cities from that nation. During the ensuing years, Wu Qi kept the West River safe and prosperous. He blocked the Ch'in kingdom's eastward expansion into the central plains.

The Elite Warrior Corps (Wu Ju Zhi)

Wu Qi was the first person in recorded history to create a national system for training and maintaining a standing professional army. His goal was to build a proficient standing army to replace the mercenaries and conscripts that filled the ranks of the army of the time. Wu set a physical standard for candidates to be accepted into his Elite Warrior Corps. Once enrolled in the system, an individual had to prepare and pass the endurance test. For the test, the candidate had to be in full armor, which entailed a metal helmet, upper body armor, hip armor, and waist armor. Body armor was made of leather, lacquer, cloth, and hemp rope. He needed to carry all the requisite weapons including a halberd, a sword, a large bow with a draw of 12 stone (about 360 pounds), a full quiver of 50 arrows, plus three days of dried rations. Then he had to march 100 li's (40 kilometers) in half a day. Once a soldier passed the test and was accepted into the Elite Warrior Corps, he became a full-time soldier. Outstanding individuals were promoted to officer rank.

In addition, Wu Qi assigned all the soldiers to specific sub-units of his Elite Warrior Corps according to their individual talents and expertise. This was equivalent to the specialized branches of service in the modern military. Men were assigned to standard infantry units, archery units, scaling/climbing units, scouts, cavalry, chariots, and so forth, according to their skills.

Wu Qi then drilled the men in marching and fighting formations and responding to commands issued via drums, gongs, flags, or signal arrows. The system promoted esprit-de-corps, unit cohesion, and comradery among the men.

The Elite Warrior Corps' all-volunteer army eliminated the need for mercenaries and conscripts. In times of national emergency, when it became necessary for a national mobilization, the professional soldiers formed the core of the citizen army to meet the foreign threat.

He treated the Elite Warriors Corps with special care and extreme discipline. Members of the corps were exempted from taxes, and their families were excused from labor levies to the realm. However, rule breakers received severe punishment.

At the onset of one battle, an Elite Warrior charged the enemy ranks without orders and succeeded in disrupting the enemy formation. His independent assault provided an opening for Wu Qi to exploit the situation and win the battle. Afterward, the soldier brought forth heads he had taken to claim his reward. Wu Qi had the man arrested. "You are a brave warrior, and your individual initiative contributed to our victory. But you acted without orders, which is a capital offense. For that you shall die; however, rest assured, your family will be well taken care of." The soldier was then beheaded.

During his tenure at the West River, Wu Qi fought seventy-six major campaigns and won sixty-four decisive victories, without suffering a single defeat.

While on the march, he always shared the men's hardship. One time a soldier suffering an open sore found his commander sucking out the puss with his own mouth. When the soldier's mother heard of the incident, she started weeping. A puzzled friend asked her why she was crying when she should be proud and happy that the general took such personal care of her son. The woman sobbed, "Yes, I know the general takes great care of his men. My husband suffered the same ailment as his son, and the general treated him in the same manner. In gratitude, my husband fought bravely and died for the general. Now I am afraid my son will follow in his father's footsteps."

Wu Qi Returns to the Court

After twelve years Lord Wen passed away and his son, Lord Wu, became ruler of the Wei kingdom. Wu Qi returned to the royal court from the West River to attend the ascension ceremony. Once again, Wu Chi's character flaws raised their ugly heads. This time, his pride and arrogance came to the fore.

Wu Qi felt that his accomplishments at the West River had earned him the right to be the prime minister. Instead, Duke Wu appointed Tien Wen to the said position.

Wu Qi left the court in frustration and intercepted the new prime minister at the palace entrance. Wu Qi approached Tien Wen, "Sir, do you know of my accomplishments? I would like to discuss them with you."

"I await your wisdom."

"I commanded armies, and I inspired the men to rise at the beat of war drums to risk their lives for the country. Can you surpass me in that?"

"No, I am not so capable in that respect."

"I governed hundreds of officials, cared for tens of thousands of people, and filled the national coffers. Can you do it better than me?"

Again, the prime minister shook his head, "No, I cannot."

"I guarded the West River territory and kept the Ch'in army at bay for twelve years, and gained thousands of *li*'s of territory. Can you accomplish that?"

"Not as well as you can."

"Since I am better than you in all these areas, how is it that your position ranks above that of mine?"

"I am distressed to be appointed to such a high position. However, one should consider that the new lord is young, and his power has yet to be solidified. The people know him not, and some court factions are still at odds with the new regime. At this trying time, should you take charge of the country or should I?"

Wu Qi pondered nodded in acceptance of the prime minister's response, "Perhaps you are right."

"That is why I am of higher rank than you."

"But, just remember, your position shall ultimately be mine."

When Lord Wu heard of the conversation, he decided not to return the general to his post but kept him at court with no military power. However, Lord Wu did acquiesce to Wu Qi's recommendation for annual military banquets for his Elite Warriors.

At the feast, soldiers with significant combat honors sat in the front tier with rich eating utensils for dining. Those with minor honors sat in the second tier with utensils of lesser value. Soldiers with no military honors sat in the last tier with utensils of least value. After the banquet, parents of military heroes received special recognition and rewards for the deeds of their sons. Emissaries from Lord Wu also distributed gifts to families of martyred soldiers. These measures raised the morale of the men, who were eager to win battle honors.

Three years later, in 389 BC, the Ch'in kingdom attacked the West River Territory with 500,000 men. Without orders from their officers, the warriors donned their armor and begged to take the field against the Ch'in invaders. Wu Qi chose 50,000 of his Elite Warriors who had sat in the third tier of the military banquets and marched to meet the enemy. In addition to the infantry, Lord Wu gave Wu Qi five hundred war chariots and 3,000 cavalrymen.

Wu Qi met the enemy at Yin-Ghin, where the Ch'in army had been besieging the city. Prior to the battle, the general exhorted his men, "An infantryman must take down an enemy infantryman, a charioteer must capture an enemy chariot and a cavalryman must bring back a counterpart of the enemy; otherwise, there will be no battle honors for you, even if we defeat the enemy."

While the Ch'in army was focused on the siege, Wu Qi marched his men behind the enemy and, on a moonless, windy night, routed the besiegers that were ten times the size of his own force.

Soon after Wu Qi's triumph at Yin-Ghin, the prime minister died and Lord Wu chose Gong Su as the new prime minister. Gong Su remembered Wu Qi's earlier confrontation with Tien Wen and was afraid the general would use his recent battle honors to contest the prime minister position.

Gong Su had married a Wei princess. He suggested that Lord Wu offer a princess to Wu Qi as a wife, to bind the general to the kingdom. Gong Su then invited Wu Qi for a banquet. During the festivities, Gong Su intentionally provoked his wife into abusing him (Gong Su) in front of his guests. As expected, the scene caused Wu Qi to turn down Lord Wu's marriage proposal, for fear of an abusive wife, which would damage his honor and reputation. The refusal caused Lord Wu to question the general's loyalty.

Again, Wu Qi had to leave his hard-earned riches and flee. By then, he had limited options. He had led armies against the powerful Ch'in and Qi kingdoms. All other kingdoms of the land, except the Chu to the south, were weaker than the Wei and thus were not ideal safe havens for Wu Qi.

Wu Qi Implements His Civil Ideas

For once, the god of fortune smiled on him. King Diao of the Chu kingdom had profound respect for Wu Chi's accomplishments. Finally, Wu Qi achieved his ambition when the King appointed him prime minister of that nation.

He got his chance to implement his nation-building ideas. He developed and, with the support of the king, implemented a grand strategy for the transformation of the government and the military system of Chu.

He dismissed hundreds of extraneous courtiers from the court. He forbade senior officials and their staff to accept bribes and peddle favors.

Royal relatives who were more than five relations distant from the king lost their stipends and had to seek their own means of subsistence. Royal relatives who were five relations or closer to the king received incrementally lower stipends, according to the proximity of their blood relation to the ruler.

Aristocrats who had inherited their positions for more than three generations were stripped of their rank and title.

These measures immediately generated a dramatic increase in the treasury from rising revenues and reduced outlays.

Concurrently, Wu Qi personally reviewed the performance and capabilities of his soldiers. He promoted men of skill and talent, which served to encourage other able individuals to join the Chu army. As Wu Qi promised, neighboring kingdoms regarded the Chu with trepidation and respect, and not one enemy army threatened the Chu border during the remainder of King Diao's reign.

Unfortunately for Wu Qi, King Diao died within a few years of the reformation. A group of dispossessed ex-officials and royal relatives took advantage of the tumultuous power transfer to launch a court revolt. They chased Wu Qi into the royal palace, where King Diao's body lay in state. With no place to escape to, Wu Qi ran up to the dead king and hugged the body for refuge. The rebels shot and hit Wu Qi with their arrows. He pulled out some of the arrows and jammed them into the king's corpse so it looked as though he had been struck by the archers. As he lay dying across the king's body, Wu Qi cried, "I may die now, but all of you will soon follow me. You have desecrated the king's body and shall pay for the crime with your own lives and those of your families."

True to Wu Qi's words, King Shu, the son of King Diao, ascended the throne and hunted down and massacred the seventy or so families that had participated in the rebellion — for attempted regicide, albeit against a king already dead. Ultimately, by choosing the location of his own death, Wu Qi posthumously took revenge on his assailants.

It should be noted that Sun Tzu's fame rests primarily on his military manual and history has recorded only one major campaign to his credit. By contrast, Wu Qi commanded troops in three kingdoms, engaged in over three scores of major conflicts, and never lost a battle.

To this date, his city, the city of Wu-Cheng, stands in north central China. And one Chinese version of the *Art of War* is called *Sun Wu Bing Fah* — meaning "Military Doctrines of Sun Tzu and Wu Qi." Wu Qi's military theories constitute the second part of that text.

It should be noted that San Yang, the aforementioned Iron Chancellor of the Ch'in reformation (See Chapter 6), served in the Wei court at the same time as Wu Qi. It was no coincidence that many of San Yang's policies at the Ch'in kingdom mirrored those practiced by Wu Qi. It was also ironic that both men died at the hands of old guard aristocrats who opposed their reform policies. The only difference was in their legacy. Wu Qi's policies were abandoned after his death, while San Yang's reforms were retained and subsequently led to the unification of China.

Although Wu Qi had greater accomplishments to his credit in comparison to his peers, Chinese historians relegated him to a role of minor significance. That was due to Wu Qi's personal character flaws which contradicted the ideals of Confucian philosophers that dominated Chinese society. A vain, greedy, and ambitious man who swore a blood oath against his own mother and murdered his own wife to advance his career was not to be glorified by Confucian scholars.

In the field, Wu Qi was the perfect commander, loved and respected by his men, and feared by his enemies. But, away from the army, he could not contain his personal shortcomings.

In the final analysis, in view of the fact that the Chu kingdom had more territory, resources, and soldiers (over a million men) than its neighbors, Wu Qi could have vanquished the other kingdoms and united China under the Chu banner; then "China" might have to be called "Chua."

Given his ambitious nature, Wu Qi might have become the Julius Caesar of the Far East. His army certainly would have placed the crown on his head. King Diao's premature death and the ensuing revolt prevented Wu Qi from achieving that.

Chapter 11. Sun Bin and 'Make Them Ride to the Sound of the Battle'

孙 膑 (战国初期)　明人绘

34. Sun Bin

Sun Bin was a scion of Sun Tzu. Some Chinese historians believe that Sun Bin might have been the true author of "The Art of War," the ancient treatise on military conflicts.

He lived in the early days of the Warring States Era. He and Pang Juan were classmates and best of friends under the tutelage of Gui Gu Zi, a legendary, perhaps mythical, sage who had trained many famous leaders of the time.

Pang Juan left the school first and became a general in the Wei kingdom. He was devious, vain, and resentful of Sun Bin's superior talent, and was afraid that one day Sun Bin would overtake him in achievement. Pang Juan invited Sun Bin to the Wei court and then framed him for treason. Sun Bin was branded as a criminal and had his kneecaps cut off as punishment. Mutilated and crippled, Sun Bin nevertheless managed to escape to the Qi kingdom.

In 354 BC, Pang Juan led the Wei army in invading the Zhao kingdom and placed its capital, Han-Dan, under siege. The King of Zhao sought help from the Qi nation. The King of Qi agreed, but, at Sun Bin's suggestion, withheld his aid for a year before dispatching his army into the fight. That maneuver allowed the two opposing armies to weaken each other.

When the Qi army took to the field, Sun Bin served as the Chief of Staff to General Tien Ji, the commander. Tien Ji had intended to march toward the fight at Han-Dan, but Sun Bin suggested otherwise. "The main strength of the Wei army is at Han-Dan. We should attack Da-Liang, the capital of the Wei kingdom. That will force the enemy to rush back to defend their capital, thus lifting the siege at Han-Dan. And we will have a well-rested army to fight a tired enemy at a location of our choosing."

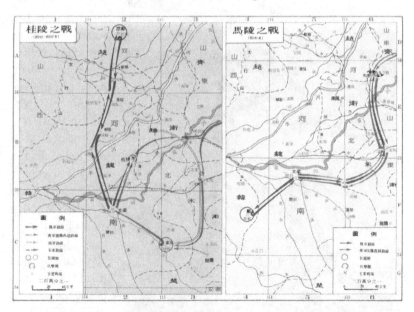

35. The Battle of Guei Ling and the Battle of Ma-Ling

The map on the left depicts the Battle of Guei Ling, with the Wei army represented by the dark (blue) line and the Qi army by the lighter (red) line. The starting point of the Wei army was in the top center of the C2 square at Da-Liang, the capital of the Wei kingdom. The army had marched north to Han-Dan (the circle at top of A2 square), which Pang Juan had taken and then abandoned when he received the recall order from Da-Liang. He rushed back to Da-Liang, then pursued the Qi army until he was ambushed at Guei-Ling (center of B2 square).

The map on the right depicts the Battle of Ma-Ling. The Wei army (dark arrow) started at Da-Liang (center top of F5 square) and attacked the Han capital of Yang-Di (circle at F4). When the Qi army attacked Da-Liang, Pang Juan led his army back to Da-Liang, then pursued the Qi army to Ma-Ling (top of E6 square), where Pang Juan was ambushed and subsequently committed suicide.

As expected, on news of the invasion by the Qi army, the King of Wei recalled Pang Juan to defend the homeland. The Wei army had already captured Han-Dan but had to abandon that city and forced-march back home. The tired Wei army attempted to chase the Qi invaders but was ambushed at Guei-Ling by the Qi army; Pang Juan was captured in the battle and then released in the ensuing peace negotiations.

Thirteen years later, in 341 BC, Pang Juan led another army of 100,000 men against the Han kingdom, which also sought aid from the Qi nation.

At Sun Bin's suggestion, the Qi kingdom promised to help the Han people fight the Wei army, but again delayed in taking any real action until the contending armies had fought five major engagements and the Han kingdom was on the brink of collapse.

General Tien Ji marched forth with 30,000 men. Once more, instead of going toward the battlefield in the Han kingdom, General Tien Ji heeded Sun Bin's advice and threatened Da-Liang. This forced Pang Juan to abandon the attack on the Han capital of Yang-Di and race back with his army to defend the Wei capital.

The moment that scouts reported the approach of Pang Juan's army, Sun Bin turned his army around and marched homeward. On the first night of the withdrawal, Sun Bin had the men build cooking fires for a 100,000 men. The second night, the number of the cooking fires dropped to 50,000; then it decreased to 30,000 on the following night.

Pang Juan had been wary of Sun Bin's maneuvers, but the dwindling number of Qi army hearth pits deceived Pang Juan into believing the Qi soldiers were deserting en masse. He abandoned his heavy infantry and pursued the Qi force with 10,000 cavalry and light infantry.

Sun Bin estimated that the Wei army would reach Ma-Ling, located in a mountain gorge, at night. He laid an ambush with 10,000 archers and crossbowmen. Sun Bin ordered trees felled to block the exit from the gorge, leaving a single tall tree standing by the side of the road. He had that tree stripped of its bark and wrote 'Pang Juan Died Under This Tree' in bold black calligraphy on the white tree trunk.

The pursuing Wei army entered the gorge and found its way blocked by fallen timber. Pang Juan went forward to investigate and saw a white tree trunk with writing on it. He ordered torches lit so he could read the inscription, and that became the signal for the Qi army to spring their ambush.

Shot full of bolts and arrows, Pang Juan lamented, "I have become the instrument of that cripple's [glorious] legacy," then drew his sword and slit his own throat.

The tired and surprised Wei army was massacred at Ma-Ling. The Qi army followed up and routed the remaining Wei soldiers. Crown Prince Sen, the Commander of the Wei main force, was captured by the victorious Qi.

The battles at Guei-Ling and Ma-Ling established Sun Bin's legacy as a premier military tactician. His strategies of 'Attack Wei to Rescue Zhao' and 'Diminishing Hearth Fires' became favorite tactics for Chinese military strategists. 'Attack Wei to Rescue Zhao' recommended avoiding 'Riding to the Sound of the Gun' and hitting key areas to force the enemy to respond to your move. 'Diminishing Hearth Fires' was a psychological misdirection to trick the enemy and hide your true strength.

It should be noted that Sun Bin applied the theories cited in "The Art of War." He chose the proper time (when the Wei army was exhausted by prolonged battle) to launch his attack. He attacked the enemy's weak point (Da-Liang), forced Pang Juan to react to the Qi maneuver, and then lured the enemy into complacency with the reduction in hearth fire strategy. Finally, he chose the place of battle to trap and annihilate the Wei army.

CHAPTER 12. ZHAO SER AND THE GREAT FAKE

In 269 BC, the Ch'in kingdom sent General Hu Yang with 100,000 men through the Han kingdom to attack the Fortress of Yu-Yu at the western edge of the Tai-Xing Mountain Range. The fortress had been built by the Zhao kingdom to defend its western border. The Han kingdom, cowed by the Ch'ins' military might, could only give muted consent to this trespassing.

King Hui Wen of the Zhao kingdom summoned his counselors for advice. Generals Lian Poh and Leh Cheng advised against sending a relief force because of the great distance (over one hundred miles) and the narrow mountain passes that had to be traversed. However, General Zhao Ser dissented. He believed it would be like 'two rats meeting in a narrow passage, the aggressive one would win the fight.' The King was persuaded by Zhao Ser's bravado and gave him the army to relieve the siege at Yu-Yu.

Zhao Ser was a distant relative of the king. He rose to prominence through his forthrightness and foresight. Initially, he served as the royal tax collector. When Duke Ping Yuan, a prominent courtier, and brother of the King, refused to pay his taxes, Zhao Ser arrested and then executed a dozen of the Duke's business managers.

Duke Ping Yuan threatened to kill Zhao Ser for the personal affront but was dissuaded by his argument for a fair and just tax system to ensure the prosperity of the kingdom. The Duke subsequently recommended Zhao Ser for a senior position in the royal court. And, Zhao Ser proved to be a capable administrator and military commander.

Strategies of Zhao Ser

From the moment of his appointment to command the army against the Ch'in invaders, Zhao Ser moved into the military cantonment to live with his troops. He distributed all the gifts and treasures he received from the King to his men. His efforts in sharing the troops' welfare endeared him to the soldiers.

Zhao Ser led his army out of Han-Dan, the capital of the Zhao kingdom, and marched southwest for ten miles, then stopped and set up camp at Fan-Wu. He ordered the men to start building a fortress and gave an unusual order; he forbade anyone from discussing military matters. The men were baffled by his lack of action, but no one dared to question his motive due to the order not to discuss military issues.

On hearing reports of the Zhao troop movement from Han-Dan, General Hu Yang sent a large detachment to attack Wu-An, a key defensive stronghold seventeen miles west of Han-Dan. The fall of Wu-An would give the Ch'in army a base from which to threaten the Zhao capital. The assault on Wu-An was a spoil attack intended to provoke a fight with Zhao Ser and tie down his army so as to prevent it from reinforcing the Zhao garrison at Yu-Yu.

Scouts reported the Ch'in army attack on Wu-An to Zhao Ser. The General did nothing to relieve the siege at Wu-An, and one of the scouts pleaded for Zhao Ser to help the defenders at Wu-An. To everyone's surprise, the General executed the scout for violating the earlier order against discussing military matters. The Zhao army continued with the fortification of its base camp and made no preparation for moving in any direction.

Since the attack on Wu-An failed to get a reaction from Zhao Ser's army, General Hu Yang sent a spy into the Zhao encampment to collect information. Zhao Ser learned of the spy's presence but did nothing to interfere with the man's activities. The spy reported the continued construction work at the Zhao encampment to the Ch'in commander. The news put Hu Yang at ease; he believed Zhao Ser was afraid to engage the Ch'in army and held his army in place, so as to defend Han-Dan, should it come under attack.

For twenty-eight days, Zhao Ser sat at Fan-Wu luring the Ch'in commander into complacency. On the twenty-ninth day, Zhao Ser ordered his men to shed their armor and then force marched for two days and one night toward Yu-Yu. The Zhao army's heavy cavalry organization enabled it to cover the one hundred miles of mountainous trail during that time frame. Zhao Ser halted seventeen miles from Yu-Yu, then set up camp to allow the army to recover from the march and prepare for battle.

Hu Yang was surprised by Zhao Ser's sudden appearance at Yu-Yu and immediately recalled the Wu-An expedition force. However, the Ch'in army lacked the mobility of the Zhao cavalry. By the time the Ch'in forces were united Zhao Ser had already fortified his position and had sent 10,000 men to seize the mountainous high ground north of Yu-Yu.

Hu Yang was trapped between three Zhao forces — the 10,000-man unit on the high ground, the Yu-Yu garrison, and Zhao Ser's main force. Hu Yang decided to assault the Zhao force atop the northern mountain because it was the smallest and the most recently established enemy position. However, the Ch'in attack was repulsed; and as the Ch'in army faltered in its assault against the high ground, Zhao Ser launched his counterattack. At the same time, the Zhao army at Yu-Yu charged out to join in the battle. Faced with attacks from three sides, the Ch'in army was annihilated.

The battle of Yu-Yu was one of the few Zhao victories against the Ch'in kingdom during the Warring States Era. The battle kept the Ch'in kingdom in check for nine years. Ironically, it set the stage for the tragic massacre at the Battle of Chang-Ping, which took place in the very same mountainous region.

Zhao Ser's victory at Yu-Yu earned him the title of Duke of Ma Fu. A mausoleum exists to this date honoring his accomplishments.

Zhao Ser was a man of foresight. His son, Zhao Gua, was considered by many to be a chip off the old block — a talented military strategist — an opinion that Zhao Ser did not share. On his deathbed, Zhao Ser warned his wife and son Zhao Gua that he should not accept a military command for it would lead to the ruin of the Zhao nation.

Seven years after the Battle at Yu-Yu, the Ch'in kingdom invaded the Han kingdom. The campaign eventually drew the Zhao army into conflict with the Ch'in invaders. (See Chapter 3. Bai Chi, the Most Successful General in Chinese History.) The struggle lasted for two years and ended with the massacre at Chang-Ping. Zhao Ser's deathbed warning proved prophetic. Zhao Gua and his army of 400,000 died in the very same mountains where his father had achieved fame nine years earlier.

Chapter 13. Yu Xu and Deception, Deception and More Deception

Four hundred and fifty-six years after Sun Bin's victory at Ma-Ling, another general used a variation of the 'Diminishing Hearth Fires' strategy to deceive and then defeat his enemy.

In the year 115, tens of thousands of Tibetan tribesmen invaded northwestern China. The Dowager Empress Zheng of the Han Empire sent Yu Xu with 3,000 men to reinforce the garrison in the Wu Du region, which was being hard pressed by the Tibetan invaders.

The Tibetans learned of Yu Xu's approach and sent 2,000 men to block a mountain pass at Xiao Shan. On learning of the enemy's disposition, Yu Xu halted his army and then spread the word that he had sent for reinforcements and would wait for their arrival before continuing his advance.

The ruse fooled the Tibetan commander at the pass into believing that Yu Xu would stay put for a while; therefore, the Tibetan chief left a small force to keep watch over Yu Xu's army while he led the rest of the army in raiding nearby Chinese townships.

Yu Xu used the opportunity to force-march his men thirty miles a day toward Wu-Du. On the first night, Yu Xu had his men dig twice the amount of cooking pits necessary for the army. The number of hearth fires doubled again each night afterward. His speed of travel prevented the Tibetan pursuers from getting a close look at the true strength of the Han army. Surveys of abandoned campsites revealed a drastic increase in the number of hearth fire pits, indicating that Yu Xu had received a great infusion of reinforcements. The ruse kept the Tibetans at a distance from the Han army, allowing Yu Xu to reach his assigned post unmolested.

Arriving at Wu-Du, Yu Xu had fewer than 3,000 men to defend the city of Chi-Ting against 20,000 Tibetans. After ten days of siege, he noticed a slackening in Tibetan attacks. Yu Xu ordered his men to use the weaker, light crossbows. The shorter range and the lessened effectiveness of the small crossbows emboldened the Tibetans, who resumed their attacks with ferocity. Yu Xu then used teams of twenty archers and heavy crossbowmen to shoot at individual enemy soldiers identified by the archer team leader. Each and every targeted Tibetan leader died under the concentrated fire of the Han killer teams. When the shaken Tibetans recoiled from their attacks, Yu Xu followed up by charging his army at the enemy, forcing them into retreat.

However, Yu Xu thought his counterattack might have revealed the limited number of Han soldiers in the city. If the Tibetans found out about the disparity in strength, it would embolden the attackers. To disguise his weakness, Yu Xu paraded his men out of the city's east gate in a long column, then returned via the north gate. The men changed to uniforms of a different color, then marched out from the north gate and reentered the city by another gate. The charade was repeated for several days, which convinced the Tibetans of the Han army's inflated strength. The fictitious number of Han soldiers was supported by the previous reports of large numbers of hearth fires left at Han army encampments.

The Tibetan commander decided to retire from the field, but at a river crossing they fell victim to another surprise. Anticipating the route of the Tibetan withdrawal, Yu Xu had prepositioned five hundred men there to ambush the enemy. That last defeat ended the Tibetan threat to the Han border.

Yu Xu's Tibetan campaign was unique in that everything went according to his plans. It was one of the few military campaigns that defied German strategist Helmut von Moltke's military axiom — "No battle plan survives contact with the enemy." Without deviation, Yu Xu devised and successfully executed his battle plan to defeat an enemy that was almost ten times his own strength.

CHAPTER 14. XIANG YU AND THE STRATEGY OF SMASHED STOVES AND SUNKEN SHIPS

36. Xiang Yu

In 209 BC, a detachment of 900 Imperial Ch'in soldiers faced death for reporting late for duty due to inclement weather. Instead of meekly accept death, two of the men killed the three officers commanding the unit, then launched a revolt against the Imperial Emperor. They failed, but they lit the spark that ignited a revolution which toppled the Imperial Ch'in Dynasty. It had

been less than 20 years since the First Emperor united the land to create the Ch'in Empire; numerous scions of the Warring States kingdoms rose up to join the rebellion. King Huai of Chu led the most powerful rebel group, and his favorite general was Xiang Liang.

In the following year, the loyalist General Zhang Han led 200,000 men and crushed the Chu resistance force at Ding-Tao (south of the Yellow River) and killed Xiang Liang. Zhang thought the remnant Chu army no longer posed a threat, so he hurried north, crossed the Yellow River, and joined forces with the 200,000-man Ch'in force under General Wang Li to fight another rebel force at Han-Dan. The rebel Zhao army at Han-Dan retreated to the city of Ju-Lu, then pleaded for help from the other rebel forces. Zhang Han left Wang Li with 200,000 men to besiege the Zhao army while he moved to the south to guard the supply line for Wang Li.

The rebel reinforcements arrived at Ju-Lu but were afraid to engage the Ch'in army. King Huai of Chu sent General Song Yi with 50,000 men to rescue the Zhao army at Ju-Lu; Xiang Yu, the nephew of Xiang Liang, was the Deputy Commander of the Chu army. Song Yi marched his army to An-Yang (about 250 km south of Ju-Lu) and went into encampment. Xiang Yu wanted to attack and avenge his uncle, but Song Yi refused. He wanted the Zhao army and the other rebel forces to fight the Ch'in army before committing his force to pick up the pieces. The Chu army sat on its heel for 46 days before Xiang Yu took matters into his own hands.

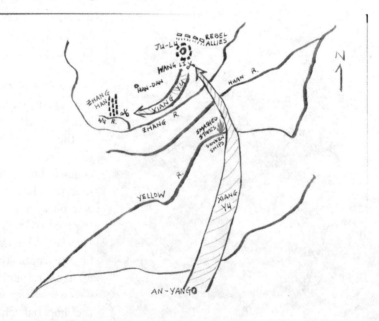

37. Battle of Ju-Lu

Xiang Yu killed Song Yi and took command of the army. In December 208 BC, Xiang Yu crossed the Yellow River and then ordered his men to sink their ships, destroy their cooking stoves and burn all excess supplies. This demonstrated his determination for victory and inspired his men to fight to the death. With only three days of rations, the Chu army marched toward Ju-Lu which was 30 miles away.

At Ju-Lu, Wang Li had 200,000 men, but they were spread out in a siege line against the Zhao force in the city in addition to being deployed to guard against the other rebel allies that had arrived on the scene earlier. The allied rebels watched as the Chu army charged into the numerically superior Ch'in army. The Chu army charged nine times and when the dust settled, Xiang Yu's men had destroyed Wang Li's army and captured the Ch'in general. Meanwhile, Zhang Han was too far away, with his army scattered along the Ch'in supply route.

After the battle, Xiang Yu became the accepted chief warlord of all the rebel forces. He marshaled the rebel alliance and turned west toward Zhang Han's army, which had been guarding the supply line for Wang Li. Xiang Yu first sent an army across the Zhang River to cut his enemy's route of withdrawal, then attacked and defeated Zhang Han at the east bank of the Wu River. Zhang Han sent for help from Xian-Yang, but none came. In the summer of 207 BC, Zhang surrendered to Xiang Yu, which spelled the beginning of the end of the Ch'in Dynasty because there was no other viable loyalist force left to defend the Ch'in Empire.

"Smashed Stoves and Sunken Ships" became a well-known byword for an all-or-nothing effort. Ironically, Xiang Yu had used the same strategy employed by the famous Ch'in general Bai Chi 70 years earlier. When Bai Chi attacked the Chu kingdom, he marched without supply trains and burned bridges and shipping along the way to demonstrate his determination for victory. Bai Chi's victory started the downfall of the Chu kingdom, and Xiang Yu's Chu army returned the favor with the same strategy to smash the Ch'in Dynasty. Within a year, Xiang Yu sacked Xiang Yang, killed the Ch'in Emperor and ended that dynasty.

Chapter 15. The Peasant and the Warrior: The Founding of the Imperial Han Empire

38. Liu Bang — The Peasant

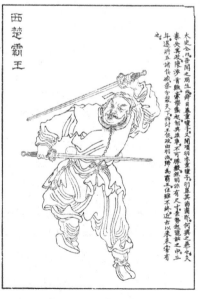

39. Xiang Yu — The Warrior

In the summer of 207 BC, General Xiang Yu defeated two Imperial Ch'in forces which totaled 400,000 men. It was the beginning of the end of the

Ch'in Dynasty. Two rebel leaders emerged as contenders for the realm — Liu Bang and Xiang Yu.

Xiang Yu was an iconic Chinese hero; a brave, fierce, aristocratic warrior and charismatic leader, loved by his men while feared by his enemies. He was given the title War Lord King of Western Chu. Xiang Yu was forthright, confident, and always led the charge through any obstacles to achieve his goals. However, he was also aloof, lacking in humility, and strong-willed, and rarely accepted counsel from others; that last trait often drove able subordinates away from his side. As a commander, he was aggressive and decisive in battle; he drove his men hard and was merciless towards his enemies. After the battle of Ju-Lu, he absorbed 200,000 Ch'in prisoners into his army. The new men were ridiculed and abused by veteran Chu soldiers, many of whom had previously suffered under the harsh rules and regulations of the Ch'in government. The new men complained about their mistreatment, which caused Xiang Yu to question their loyalty. He massacred all 200,000 ex-prisoners.

In contrast, Liu Bang was a commoner with the street wiles of a survivalist. He attracted men from all walks of life into his service. He surrounded himself with able men and relied on their advice to resolve problems. Many men who abandoned Xiang Yu became able leaders in Liu Bang's camp and he made maximum use of his subordinates' talents.

The greater rebel alliance against the Ch'in Empire was under the nominal leadership of King Huai, a royal descendant of the Chu kingdom of the Warring States Era. He promised a kingship to any rebel leader who captured Xian-Yang, the Ch'in capital.

In the ensuing struggles, the tactical strategies of Liu Bang and Xiang Yu reflected their personalities. Xiang Yu attacked his enemies with abandon and often massacred his opponents' armies, whereas Liu Bang preceded force with diplomacy, and often persuaded his enemies to surrender. When force was required, he usually struck strategic weak points to achieve tactical advantage and victory.

Aggressive attacks by Xiang Yu drew the bulk of the Ch'in loyalist army to fight against him, often to the bitter end. Liu Bang, on the other hand, took advantage of the weakened Ch'in positions and often negotiated the surrender of the opposition in order to succeed with minimal resistance, thus ending the reign of the Ch'in dynasty.

When Liu Bang entered Xian-Yang, the capital, he forbade sacking of the city, kept the Ch'in treasury intact, and replaced the oppressive Ch'in laws with three simple rules: Murderers will be executed; thieves and robbers will be punished; injuries committed against another person will be punished. All other Ch'in laws were abolished. However, he retained the administrative structure of the Ch'in government to maintain public order. His humane measures won the support of the people.

Despite having lost the race to capture Xian-Yang, Xiang Yu refused to acknowledge Liu Bang's primacy as the leader of the rebel force. Xiang Yu forced his way into Xian-Yang and executed Tzu Ying, the last emperor of the Ch'in dynasty who had previously surrendered to Liu Bang, then torched the Imperial Palace and massacred the city's populace. The palace fire burned for three months, which destroyed, among other things, the Ch'ins' Imperial collection of books and historical records; it was akin to Caesar's burning of the Egyptian Library at Alexandria in 48 BC.

In the ensuing lull, Xiang Yu proclaimed himself King of Chu and installed Liu Bang as King of the Han region in western China. Liu accepted the position because he was not yet ready to confront Xiang Yu. Other rebel warlords also received fiefdoms from Xiang Yu. The ensuing peace was but a temporary respite; soon, the realm reverted to the political landscape of the Warring States Era, with the warlords fighting each other for supremacy over the empire. Xiang Yu and Liu Bang were the primary opponents, while the other warlords changed sides as the situation suited their political ends.

The following year, Xiang Yu was often victorious against Liu Bang, but Liu Bang always managed to escape and return to the fight. During one of his flights from Xiang Yu, Liu Bang was in such a hurry to escape that he pushed his own son out of his chariot three times to lighten the load; and three times his staff rescued the boy. Xiang Yu captured Liu Bang's parents and wife and threatened to boil them into the soup if Liu did not surrender. Liu still refused to give in. In the end, he was able to form an alliance with the other rebel leaders to band together against Xiang Yu, who was the strongest of the rebel forces.

In spite of his temper, Xiang Yu behaved with a sense of honor in dealing with Liu Bang. He did not boil Liu's family as he had threatened. At another time, during their power struggle, Liu Bang was forced to visit Xiang Yu at Hong-Meng for negotiations. Xiang Yu's staff suggested that he kill Liu Bang at the banquet dinner, but Xiang Yu refused to dishonor himself by resorting to murder of a former ally to whom he had promised safe passage. Xiang Yu went on to win every battle against his foes, except for the last one.

The two great armies fought to a standstill at the Hong Gou River. After two years of standoff, in 203 BC, at Liu Bang's initiative, the two sides concluded a peace accord. They divided the empire into two parts with the Hong Gou River as the border. Liu Bang would rule the western lands, while Xiang Yu kept the eastern territories. At the same time, Liu Bang got his family back, alive.

Xiang Yu assembled his army and marched eastward. But the peace accord had been a ruse. Liu summoned help from his allies and launched an attack against the Xiang Yu's withdrawing Chu force. But the allies did not show up and Liu had to fight Xiang Yu alone. Furious counterattacks by Xiang Yu forced Liu to retreat. In desperation, Liu promised kingships to the other warlords, which induced them to join the fight against Xiang Yu.

Meanwhile, Xiang Yu had retreated to Gai-Xia due to lack of supplies. Liu Bang and his allies had 300,000 men against Xiang Yu's 100,000. Liu Bang used Fabian strategy by sending detachments to cut Xiang Yu's supply lines, then placed Han Xin, one of the warlords, in command of the combined army in a showdown with Xiang Yu.

Han Xin deployed his men like Hannibal at the Battle of Cannae — except Han had three times the force of his opponent. As expected, Xiang Yu sent his army charging into the center of the allied forces. Han Xin waited until the Chu army was fully engaged and deep in the allied pocket before he sent in the two wings against Xiang Yu's flank. Xiang Yu was finally defeated, but he managed to disengage and withdrew with 50,000 men.

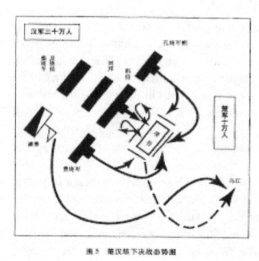

图 5 楚汉垓下决战态势图

40. Battle of Gai Xia: Xiang Yu (100,000 men, White block); Liu Bang (300,000 men, Black blocks).

Liu was worried that Xiang Yu might escape to his home base (the Chu territory) east of the Yangtze River. Liu Bang ordered his men to learn to sing. That evening, Xiang Yu and his men found themselves besieged by songs from all sides. The Han army sang songs of the Chu region, where Xiang Yu had recruited most of his troops. The chorus of Chu songs from the enemy camps shocked and demoralized Xiang Yu and his men. It convinced the King of Chu that Liu had already captured his (Xiang Yu's) homeland and that many of his men had surrendered to Liu Bang.

Despondent, the mightiest warrior of the land lost heart and gave up the fight. He disbanded his men and allowed them to head for home, then returned to his tent. There, he wrote his own requiem poem while he drank and danced with his favorite concubine Yu Ji.

41. Xiang Yu and Yu Ji — The Last Dance

垓下歌　‧　項羽
　力拔山兮氣蓋世
　時不利兮騅不逝
　騅不逝兮可奈何
　虞兮虞兮奈若何

Lament at Gai-Xia by Xiang Yu

Powerful as a mountain with ability higher than the sky,
Alas, the time is not right and Zhui goes not forth.
Zhui goes not forth and what can I do,
Yu Ji, oh Yu Ji, what shall I do (with thee)?
(Zhui was Xiang Yu's favorite war horse that he always rode into battle.)

After Xiang Yu sang his poem, Yu Ji realized the end was near. She drew a sword and committed suicide to avoid abuse by the Han army. Tearfully, Xiang Yu buried Yu Ji, then took the 800 men who chose to remain with him and rode south in a breakout. They escaped undetected through the allied encirclements, but at dawn, a 5,000-man Han cavalry force was in hot pursuit.

Xiang Yu's party lost their way in the fen and stopped to ask a farmer for direction. The farmer recognized the King of Chu as the man responsible for the recent killings and sufferings. He (the farmer) deliberately misdirected them into the marshlands. By the time Xiang Yu realized the error and doubled back, the pursuers had caught up and trapped the general at the shore of Wu River. By then, he had only 26 men left out of the original force of 100,000 before the battle.

A ferryman offered to take Xiang Yu across the river, but the King of Chu refused to leave his men behind. He dismounted and gave his steed, Zhui, to the ferryman, then led his remaining 26 men in an infantry charge against the pursuers. Finally, with multiple wounds, Xiang Yu slit his own throat; the would-be emperor was only 31.

As a commander, Xiang Yu was very much like Alexander the Great. Xiang Yu was charismatic, loved by his men and feared by his enemies. He was fearless in battle, always led from the front, and often won battles against overwhelming odds. Unfortunately, he won every battle except the last one.

42. Xiang Yu's suicide at the bank of the Wu River

After Xiang Yu died, Liu Bang created the Imperial Han Dynasty and installed his former allies as kings. The name for the ethnic Han race of China originated from his dynasty. He was also the first of only two commoners to ever become the Emperor of China.

In the final analysis, the brave and honorable aristocratic champion warrior was vanquished by the lowly but wily, scheming and pragmatic peasant. The difference between victory and defeat was due to their leadership styles. Xiang Yu's courage and martial skills inspired loyalty and respect from his men and struck fear into his enemies. He was a battering ram that smashed everything that stood in his path. However, his youthful vitality made him overconfident and arrogant; he lacked the humility and maturity to accept advice from his staff, which often drove them away and into the arms of his opponents. He was undone by his own misplaced sense of honor and justice.

Liu Bang, on the other hand, was practical and street wise. He accepted and welcomed all sorts of people into his service; many members of his staff were former subordinates of Xiang Yu. Liu Bang heeded the counsel of his advisors for they knew Xiang Yu's strengths and weaknesses, and they helped shape the strategy that defeated the aristocratic general. Most important of all, Liu did not allow ethics and morals to stand in the way of his goal — victory. To Liu Bang, the end justified the means.

In this case, pragmatism and wiles triumphed over chivalry and righteousness.

Chapter 16. The Bare Head Brigade, Berserker Troops of Ancient China

43. Terracotta warriors and an officer of the Bare Head Brigade from the tomb of the First Emperor of China, Xi-An, Shaan Xi Province, China.
Note the differences in hair styles that distinguished the officer from the men.

Shaped of terracotta or earthenware clay, ranks of soldiers with neither helmets nor armor, wearing only battle tunics, stand at the front ranks of the Ch'in army in the First Emperor's tomb at Xi-An, Shaanxi Province, China. They represent the berserker troops of the Imperial Ch'in (Qin) Dynasty, better known as the Bare Head Brigade.

China has an extensive military history. The first empire (Ch'in) was the product of five hundred plus years of incessant warfare during the Spring and Autumn Era (770–476 BC) and the ensuing Warring States Era (476–221 BC). At the time, seven powerful kingdoms dominated central China — Ch'in, Qi, Chu, Yan, Han, Zhao and Wei. Initially, the Ch'in was neither the largest nor the strongest of those seven. In 358 BC, Chancellor San Yang (395–338 BC) initiated a reformation that changed everything. His political, economic, and military policies transformed the Ch'in kingdom from a barbaric backwater state to a first rate power that ultimately conquered the other kingdoms to create the Ch'in Empire, which subsequently evolved into the modern day China.

Earlier in his career, San had served with Wu Qi in the royal court of the Wei kingdom. (see chapter on Wu Qi, The Flawed Perfect General.) San was impressed with the way Wu reformed the Wei army, especially the Elite Warrior Corps, and its successes on the battlefield. As the Chancellor of the Ch'in kingdom, San set out to create a unique fighting force that he named *Ke Tou Jun*, The Bare Head Brigade. The men of the unit wore only battle tunics into battle.

To motivate the men, San decreed that a Bare Head soldier who took the head of an enemy officer was promoted one rank, given a hectare of farmland, and nine *mu* of land for building a house. He was also eligible for promotion to the officer rank. Should the soldier perish in battle, his rewards were passed on to his family. Battle honors won could also be used to defray punishments of criminal wrongs committed by family members.

San Yang's reward system compared favorably to that of the other kingdoms of the time. For example, the neighboring Wei state paid only eight copper coins for each enemy head taken on the battlefield. The Ch'in system motivated men to seek combat for riches and fame. On hearing news of an oncoming military campaign, men often congratulated each other for the opportunity of a financial windfall. It was also a way for commoners to enter the ranks of the aristocratic elite — through battle honors. There were 23 ranks for a common soldier to be promoted into. Along with military promotions came wealth, prestige and political advancement. Of course, that is if the individual survived the ordeal.

44. Top view of the vanguard of Battle Formation in No. 1 Pit, Tomb of the First Emperor. Note armored warriors positioned behind the unarmored Bare Head warriors in battle tunics.

Warriors of the Bare Head Brigade were at the forefront of the battles that finally united China in 221 BC. They relied on speed, violence, and fierce fighting spirit to destroy their enemies; that and the psychological effect of their reputation which demoralized their foes even before the onset of the battle. The officers who led them were similarly attired. The emphasis on speed and agility precluded the use of shields. That was why in the First

Emperor's tomb no warrior in battle tunic carried a shield, and certainly not the officers. Chinese officers, as a rule, do not use shields.

45. Side view of the vanguard of Battle Formation in No. 1 Pit, Tomb of the First Emperor. Note armored warriors positioned behind the unarmored Bare Head warriors in battle tunics.

The Bare Head warriors were comparable to Viking berserkers in terms of aggressiveness and ferocity; but, that was where the similarities ended. The Chinese warriors wore no armor or helmet and fought as a disciplined arm of a large army. In battle, they were supported by archers and crossbowmen. They numbered in the tens of thousands and were organized in regiment-sized units. They were also well rewarded for their valor. Finally, a Viking war leader did not have to lose his head if his men failed to do their job.

Tactically, the Bare Head Brigade did not initiate battles except in surprise raids and ambushes. The Ch'in army standard tactic was to fire crossbows at a distance of 150 paces. Some of the crossbowmen were armed with the repeating crossbow (*Lian Huan Nu*) that fired ten bolts in fifteen seconds. The *Lian Huan Nu* was not an accurate weapon, but there is quality in numbers when you have 10,000 crossbowmen; plus, the poisonous tips of the bolts increased their lethal effect. At sixty paces, archers used their bows and arrows, which were slower in firing than the repeating crossbows but more accurate. The archers stood three ranks deep and fired sequentially by rank, raining a continuous hail of missiles upon the enemy. Finally, when the army closed to within twenty paces of the enemy, the missiles stopped and the shock troops, the Bare Head Brigade, charged forward to finish off the enemy.

The short distance that Bare Head warriors had to cover to reach the enemy reduced the risks and the casualty rate of the unarmored warriors. Some men even fought bare-chested. Historical records described one survivor's account of an encounter with the Bare Head Brigade: 'One Bare Head demon soldier swung his sword and lopped off the head of an unfortunate officer; he snatched up the head by its hair knot, then kicked another officer to his knees. Before that officer could react, he found his neck locked under the armpit of the demon warrior from whose hand dangled the recently severed head, which repeatedly swung and banged against the captive officer's face. That Bare Head soldier then continued charging at the enemy, even as he held onto to his gruesome trophy and all the while dragging his screaming captive under his armpit.'

At the end of a battle, each junior officer from centurion on down had to submit at least one severed head to be credited to his unit, preferably that of an enemy officer; or the Ch'in officer would lose his head himself. Junior officers whose unit turned in thirty-two heads or more were eligible for one grade promotion.

The unification of China in 221 BC spelled the end of the Bare Head Brigade. There was no longer a need for a large standing army, and with no suitable foes, the Bare Head Brigade became a casualty of peace. In addition, the existence of such an elite fighting force posed a potential threat to the realm and the emperor. Finally, the First Emperor instituted the Mandarin bureaucracy to rule his realm, which ended the path for political advancement by common soldiers through martial feats on the battlefield.

In the ensuing Chinese dynasties, other elite military units cropped up, but none were comparable to the Bare Head Brigade in terms of fame and ferocity. Today, their memory is kept alive through their terracotta statues, where they remain as eternal guardians for their Emperor.

Chapter 17. Psychological Warfare, 285 BC

46. The Charge of the Bulls at Jih-Moh

"Know thy enemy and know thy self, you shall persevere in all your battles." — *The Art of War*, Sun Tzu (circa 500 BC).

The essence of the above statement lies in the psychological preparation of the battlefield in order to maneuver and weaken the foe by attacks on the mental plane.

One of the earliest and most notable recorded examples of psychological warfare took place in China in 285 BC, between the armies of the Yan and Qi nations in the northeastern Shantung Province of modern day China.

The outcome of the campaign was not decided on the field of battle but by the mental strategy of the opposing commanders, using psychological weaponry. Leaders on both sides employed significant efforts to influence the minds of the soldiers, the civilian populace, and the opposing royal courts. In no other battle in human history has psychology played such a crucial role in deciding the outcome.

* * *

In 285 BC, while Rome was in the budding stage of its development into an empire, China entered the final phase of the Warring States Era (476–221 BC). Seven major military powers, the Ch'in, Qi, Chu, Yan, Han, Zhao, and the Wei vied for control of the land.

Twenty-eight years earlier, King Shuan of Qi had invaded and conquered most of the Yan nation. Hui, the King of the Yan nation, had been forced to commit suicide.

The victorious Qi army plundered the land and carted away the Nine Bronze Ceremonial Urns — the symbol of authority and power of the Yan royal household — before they were driven back to the Qi nation.

Hui's son ascended to the throne and took the name of Tso as his royal appellation. For 28 years, King Tso built up his resources and prepared for revenge. He hired Leh Yi, an able military leader, to lead the Yan effort against the Qi.

Leh Yi started with the political preparation of the battlefield. He persuaded King Tso to form an alliance with the Ch'in, Zhao, Wei and Han nations to jointly attack the Qi kingdom. The allied nations fielded a powerful army and, more importantly, isolated the Qi from its two powerful neighbors — the Zhao and Wei. Those two states, had they not been allied (with the Yan kingdom), might have been swayed to come to the aid of the beleaguered Qi nation.

By this time, King Shuan of the Qi kingdom had passed away and his son King Min ruled. King Min personally led the Qi army against the grand alliance forces at the bank of the Ji River, a tributary of the Yellow River. Leh Yi led the allied armies and overwhelmed the Qi army with ease.

King Min fled to Lin Tse, the capital of the Qi nation.

Satisfied with the victory at the Ji River, the Ch'in, Wei, Zhao and Han armies plundered Qi border cities and then returned to their home states, while Leh Yi continued the attack with the Yan army.

Lin Tse and dozens of other Qi cities quickly surrendered to the Yan army. After almost 30 years of absence, the Nine Bronze Ceremonial Urns of the Yan nation were returned to their rightful owner.

King Min fled to Ghu, a city to the north of Lin Tse. Desperate for aid, Min dispatched an emissary to seek help from the Chu kingdom, the lone military power not yet involved in the conflict. Min promised all the land north of the Huai River as payment for the Chus' assistance. Meanwhile, he gathered the remnants of his army to Ghu in preparation for a siege.

The King of Chu readily agreed to rescue the beleaguered Qi nation. An army of 200,000 men marched into the Qi territory to garrison the land promised by Min and to preserve the Qi nation. Unbeknownst to Min, the King of Chu had instructed General Nao Tsi, the Chu army commander, to 'be flexible' in executing the rescue portion of the agreement.

General Nao Tsi was empowered to make decisions on all matters, so long as the outcome was beneficial to the Chu nation. The general was well aware of Leh Yi's competence, and he had no desire to risk his military reputation in the battle against the Yan army. Nao Tsi secretly sent an emissary to Leh Yi with a proposal. The Chu general promised to kill King Min and surrender the remaining Qi territories in return for half of the Qi kingdom.

Leh Yi readily agreed to the treacherous pact. His goal had been to eliminate the Qi as a nation. The agreement would accomplish his mission with no further expenditure of resources, in addition to gaining half of the Qi territory.

Nao Tsi encamped at the city of Gu-Li, then invited King Min to inspect the Chu soldiers. When the King arrived, Nao Tsi promptly massacred his entourage, then hung the King by his heels from a beam where he suffered for three days before expiring.

Nao Tsi left most of his army at Gu-Li and, accompanied by only a detachment of personal guards, marched to take control of the Ghu city. But, before he could turn the city over to Leh Yi, the Qi people at Ghu learned of Nao Tsi's treachery against their king. Qi citizens killed the Chu general and his men, then secured the city against the Chu and the Yan armies.

Prince Fa Tsang ascended to the Qi throne and continued the resistance against the Yan invaders.

The leaderless Chu army fell apart; half of the men fled home, and the rest were absorbed by Leh Yi into the Yan army.

Nao Tsi's failure to deliver Ghu and the Qi territories forced Leh Yi to resume his campaign in the Qi nation. Leh Yi remembered that 30 years ago, when the victorious Qi army overran half of the Yan kingdom, they had ravaged the Yan territories. The excesses of the Qi army at the time had prompted the Yan people to join the ranks of the Yan army, which eventually drove the Qi invaders out of the Yan nation. Leh Yi was determined not to repeat the mistakes of his enemy. He ordered humane treatment of the Qi people, reduced their taxes, and forbid the draft of forced laborers in the captured territories by the Yan army.

He took special care to safeguard the Nine Ceremonial Urns of the Qi clan at Lin Tse, honored the temples of the Qi forefathers, and provided aid and comfort to ease the burden of a populace devastated by warfare.

The Qi people welcomed Leh Yi's humanitarian measures and many of them willingly accepted Leh Yi as their governor. Within six months, the Yan army captured over 70 cities, leaving only the cities of Ghu and Jih-Moh to continue the resistance.

The commander of the Jih-Moh forces died of illness and a man named Tien Dan took over the city's defenses. Tien Dan was a royal kinsman of King Min and had been a minor official in charge of the public market at Lin Tse.

Prior to fleeing from the Yan army at Lin Tse, Tien Dan recalled the scenes of heavy traffic at the busy marketplace. He ordered servants to cut off the protruding ends of the axles of all his carriages and to reinforce and protect the spokes of the wheels with metal plates. At the time, many people laughed at Tien Dan's odd behavior. However, when the pursuing Yan army approached, Tien Dan and his clansmen made good their escape with the reinforced vehicles, while many of his compatriots were taken prisoner when their carriages were disabled, their wheels destroyed by the protruding axles of adjacent vehicles.

The people of Jih-Moh remembered the incident with the axles and were impressed with Tien Dan's foresight; they chose Tien Dan as their new commander.

Tien Dan quickly won the hearts and minds of the people of Jih-Moh. He spent his own money to improve the lot of the soldiers and labored alongside the citizenry to strengthen the city's defenses. He also sent every able-bodied member of his clan, male and female, to join the city's defense force.

For three years, defenders of the two Qi cities resisted many furious assaults by the Yan army. Leh Yi, shrewd but also frustrated, decided to change tactics. He withdrew his army to a distance of nine li's and ordered his soldiers not to detain any Qi civilian who attempted to enter or leave the cities of Jih-Moh and Ghu. The Yan soldiers befriended the Qi people, fed them and, when necessary, clothed them.

Leh Yi intended for the Qi people to accept the Yan rule and surrender the two cities without further bloodshed. In time, Leh Yi's policy removed much of the fear and animosity the Qi people had toward the Yan invaders.

The lack of armed conflict combined with Leh Yi's pacification measures posed a problem for Tien Dan. He had difficulty maintaining a strong adversarial spirit among the defenders against the Yan army.

At that bleak moment, Tien Dan's spies brought a crucial piece of information that provided a ray of hope for the Qi people. Qi Jie, an arrogant and self-centered official in the Yan court, fancied himself to be an expert military strategist. Envious of Leh Yi's success, Qi Jie aspired to command the Yan army. He befriended the Yan Crown Prince and persuaded him to petition the Yan court. "King Min of Qi died three years ago. Only the cities of Ghu and Jih-Moh remain unconquered. Why is it that Leh Yi could capture over seventy cities in six months, yet has been unable to take the last two in three years? That is because Leh Yi wants to appease the Qi people and gain their respect. Ultimately, Leh Yi wishes to make himself King of the Qi nation."

Tso, the King of Yen, did not appreciate the Crown Prince's foolish meddling in military affairs. The King grew angry with the Crown Prince who dared to question the loyalty and competence of the King's favorite general, who had brought back the clan's nine sacred urns. In a fit of rage, the King had the Crown Prince caned for his impertinence.

However, within one year, King Tso died and the Crown Prince became king.

As soon as the new king ascended to the throne, Tien Dan sent agents to spread the following rumor in the Yan Court: "Leh Yi captured over seventy Qi cities in six months, but failed to take two cities in four years. That is because Leh Yi aspires to sit on the throne of the Qi state. Out of loyalty and sworn allegiance to the old king, Leh Yi has kept his own ambition in check. The Yan army's compassionate policy has won the hearts of the Qi people, and it will only be a matter of time before Leh Yi declares himself King of the Qi nation. The Qi people are afraid that if a new Yan commander is sent to replace Leh Yi, it will spell the end of the two cities and the Qi as a nation."

This rumor affirmed the new Yan King's doubts about Leh Yi's loyalty, while memories of the caning he received fueled the King's hatred for the General. The King dispatched Qi Jie to replace Leh Yi.

Fearful of losing his life, Leh Yi fled to his homeland, the Zhao Kingdom. Leh Yi had been a popular commander, so his summary removal and the immediate revocation of all previous orders given by Leh Yi caused much disgruntlement in the Yan camp. Three days after Qi Jie assumed command, the Yan army renewed assaults on the two Qi cities.

Elated by the removal of Leh Yi, Tien Dan quickly implemented a scheme to boost the morale of the Qi defenders and at the same time erode the enemy's fighting spirit. He announced to the people of Jih-Moh, "Last night, in my dream, I encountered the Jade Emperor of Heaven. He told me the Yan army will soon be defeated and the Qi nation shall recover its lost territories. To help us achieve victory, the Jade Emperor promised to send us a Seer who will guide us to victory."

A very astute soldier approached Tien Dan and whispered in his ear, "Could I be the Seer sent by the gods?" Tien Dan quickly and cunningly presented the soldier to the people as the Seer from Heaven.

Tien Dan draped the Seer in a fine robe, seated him in the place of honor at every public gathering in the city of Jih-Moh, and treated him with the respect due to a deity. From then on, every order issued by Tien Dan was issued in the name of the Seer.

The next day, Tien Dan decreed to the people of Jih-Moh, "The Seer said everyone should make offerings to their ancestors before each meal, to gain the protection of the gods in the coming battles." Food offerings to the ancestors appeared in the courtyards and balconies of every household in Jih-Moh. The massive outdoor display of food attracted flocks of birds, which circled the sky over the city of Jih-Moh. Yan soldiers saw the strange sight, and soon the entire Yan encampment was rife with the story — 'the gods are protecting the Qi people in Jih-Moh. To fight the people of Jih-Moh is to act against the will of the Heaven." Yan soldiers lost the desire to fight and the attacks against Jih-Moh slacked off.

Tien Dan next devised a way to restore the fighting spirit of his people. He sent provocateurs to plant another rumor among the Yan. "General Leh Yi was too humane. He never killed or mistreated his captives; therefore, the Qi people were not afraid of fighting against him. If the Qi captives were to have their noses cut off, it would strike fear into the hearts of the Qi defenders."

Qi Jie had been despondent over the failure of his army to take the two cities. His insults of Leh Yi and the boasts to King Hui came vividly to mind. The Yan general fell for Tien Dan's ruse and ordered the Yan soldiers to cut off the noses of all Qi prisoners. He then paraded the noseless captives in front of the Qi. The Qi soldiers saw what had happened to their captured comrades and resolved to fight to the death against the enemy. No one wished to suffer the shame of meeting his ancestors in the afterlife with unrecognizable facial features.

Tien Dan's agents next spread the word in the Yan camp, "The graves of the Qi people's ancestors are outside of the city. If the Yan army desecrated them, it would shame and demoralize the Qi defenders."

Within days after the most recent rumor had started, Yan soldiers excavated Qi ancestral gravesites, burned the corpses, and scattered the bones. The destruction of their sacred graves enraged the Qi people. They petitioned Tien Dan to attack the hated enemy. Tien Dan agreed to attack the Yan invaders, but only after certain preparations had been made. He announced to the people, "The Seer says we need to be patient a bit longer, the moment to strike is near."

At last, satisfied with the fighting spirit of his men, Tien Dan set in motion a final series of events to deceive the enemy into lowering its vigilance. First, Tien Dan sent the old, the weak, and women in uniform to help defend the city wall. A few days later, Tien Dan requested a truce and dispatched an official envoy to the Yan camp. The emissary professed that the people of Jih-Moh had been starving and demoralized and thus would like to arrange for an auspicious date for an honorable surrender.

Qi Jie proudly announced the news of the coming surrender to his army, resulting in cheers and celebrations throughout the Yan encampment. That night, Tien Dan dispatched a group of emissaries into the Yan camp. They claimed to represent elite leaders of the city and brought gold and jewelry for Qi Jih's senior officers to purchase safety from the conquering army when the city surrendered to the victors. The Yan officers greedily accepted the bribes and handed out small pennants to mark the household to be protected from Yan soldiers.

The truce kept the Yan soldiers away from the city walls and allowed time for Tien Dan to implement the final phase of his scheme. He ordered large holes dug into the inner side of the city wall facing the Yan encampment. The laborers took care to leave a thin layer of the outer wall undamaged. Tien Dan then collected over 1,000 cattle from the city populace. Large sheets of cloth painted with bright multi-colored dragons draped the backs of the cattle. Sharp knives were tied to their horns and oil and wax soaked reeds were affixed like giant brooms to the animals' tails.

On the night before the scheduled surrender of Jih-Moh, Tien Dan assembled 5,000 elite soldiers. He painted their faces in the same colors and patterns that adorned the cloth on the cattle. Each soldier held a walnut in his mouth to remind him to be quiet. At midnight, laborers broke through the city wall at the previously semi hollowed areas. Soldiers then drove the cattle through the tunnels and lit the reeds tied to their tails. Panicked by the fire and in pain, the cattle charged into the Yan encampment, followed by the 5,000 Qi soldiers.

The men of the Yan encampment had been celebrating in anticipation of the following day's surrender of Jih-Moh. Thousands of thundering hoofs and bellows of animals in pain awakened the bleary-eyed Yan soldiers. It appeared as if an army of dragons was charging and spitting flames in the Yan encampment. The 1,000 plus broom-sized torches lit up the night. Anyone in the path of the cattle was gored or trampled. The blazing brooms set the landscape and the encampment on fire. From the dancing shadows of the fiery flames emerged 5,000 silent, devil-like warriors wielding big knives and battle-axes charging into the fray. The men and women on the Jih-Moh battlements, exhilarated to be finally on the offensive, wanted to participate in the attack against the hated enemy. They beat drums and banged metals utensils to add to the din of the battle.

Yan soldiers had heard about the seer sent by the gods to help the Qi people. The sight of flaming dragons and devil warriors struck fear into the hearts of the Yan troops. The surprise was total; no Yan officer attempted to organize a defense of the camp. Yan soldiers were more concerned with fleeing than fighting.

Behind the 5,000 painted warriors, Tien Dan led the remainder of the army and pressed home the attack. Qi Jih died while trying to escape.

The victory at Jih-Moh and the death of the Yan Commander incited other Qi cities to revolt against their conquerors. In no time, Tien Dan had restored the Qi border.

The grateful people of the Qi nation offered Tien Dan the royal crown. Tien Dan refused; he acknowledged the rule of his nephew, King Hsiang. In appreciation for his loyalty, the King appointed Tien Dan as the Prime Minister.

CHAPTER 18. THE BATTLE OF THE RED CLIFF, THE SALAMIS OF ANCIENT CHINA

47. Red Cliff

In the year 208, the Han imperial dynasty which had ruled China for almost 400 years had finally crumbled, with warlords teeming across the land. Emperor Xian became a puppet under the thumb of his Prime Minister

Cao Cao (AD 155–220). By autumn of that year, Cao Cao had vanquished all the warlords in the northern part of the Han Empire and then pointed his army southward to complete the reunification of the realm.

Two warlords stood in the way of Cao Cao's goal. Liu Biao ruled Jing-Zhou, a strategic province on the northern bank of the Yangtze River. From his naval base at Jiang-Ling, Liu Biao controlled the center stretch of the Yangtze. Sun Quan, the other warlord, ruled the territory south of the Yangtze River.

As Cao Cao marched south, Liu Biao had fortuitously died of illness, leaving his younger son Liu Cong in charge. The Liu army had been weakened by continuous warfare against Sun Quan and thus was in no shape to resist Cao Cao. Liu Cong surrendered without a fight; however, one of his father's retainers, Liu Bei, a distant relative of the Han Emperor, refused to kneel to Cao Cao. Liu Bei's force was overwhelmed at the battle of Chang-Ban and subsequently fled south with 20,000 men.

Liu Bei eventually formed an alliance with Sun Quan to oppose Cao Cao's juggernaut. The Southern Alliance had 50,000 men against Cao Cao's force of 800,000, which had been expanded to an army of a million men.

Cao Cao had the numerical edge, but his army also had several disadvantages; its soldiers were mostly northern infantry and cavalrymen, not familiar with maritime warfare or boats in general; second, they had been campaigning in the north and were worn out from the extended time in the field; third, they were not used to the swampy terrain and climate in the south, and many men fell ill; fourth, it was near winter and supplies were not readily available. However, Cao Cao did have Liu Biao's navy which had been absorbed into the invasion force.

Cao Cao's hope for a quick victory was dashed when his vanguard fleet was defeated by Sun Quan's navy at Xia-Kou and had to retreat to Wu-Lin.

While Cao Cao's soldiers trained to fight aboard ships, Pang Tong, a defector from the Southern Alliance, suggested that the northern army link its ships together with chains, then place planks across the decks to reduce the wave motion and form stable platforms for fighting the enemy. Cao Cao accepted the idea, and his ships became floating fortresses.

On a foggy night, a flotilla from the south sailed toward Wu-Lin. The men aboard the southern boats beat drums and shouted as if they were making a night raid. Cao Cao did not want to risk his navy fighting in the fog, so he ordered his men to shoot arrows at the night raiders. When the fog lifted, the southern sailors sailed back, but not before shouting their "appreciations for the gift of arrows," which had covered the straw men that had been neatly arranged on the sides of the boats. Over 100,000 arrows were collected from the straw dummies aboard the boats.

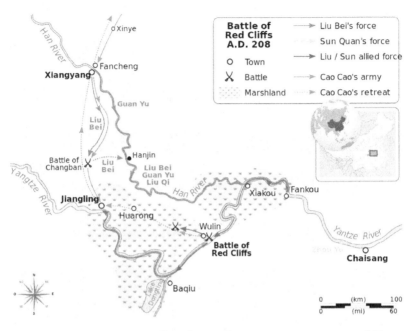

However, not all was well in the southern encampment. General Huang Guy, the commander of Sun Quan's naval forces, suggested that they pursue a negotiated peace with the numerically superior enemy. For his defeatist position, Huang Guy was caned viciously. A few days later, Huang Guy sent a messenger to Cao Cao, offering to surrender his command to the northern invaders. Cao Cao accepted the offer when his spies confirmed that Huang Guy had indeed been punished for his desire for a negotiated peace.

A few days later, when the wind shifted from east to west, a fleet of ten Wu navy ships flying the agreed upon red banners sailed up the Yangtze River toward Wu-Lin. Cao Cao's men crowded their ships and cheered at the approaching fleet of Huang Guy. They watched as the defecting ships sailed within a kilometer of Cao Cao's naval base, whereupon, to their horror, sailors aboard the Wu fleet torched their own ships before leaping into small boats and sailing back down the river.

The ten flaming ships rammed into the northern fleet, whose ships were chained together thus unable to maneuver. Cao Cao realized too late that the defection had been a ruse. In fact, Pang Tong's suggestion for linking the ships together had also been engineered by the Southern Alliance, for Pang Tong had escaped from Cao Cao's camp at the same time the ruse was executed.

As the northern ships burned, another Southern Alliance fleet appeared on the horizon and launched its attack. Cao Cao escaped ashore; then made a hasty retreat back north. Along the way, his army was ambushed by pre-positioned Southern Alliance forces.

Cao Cao would have been captured by the alliance forces at the Hua-Rong Pass, had not General Guan Yu let Cao Cao get away. Years earlier, Cao Cao had captured Guan Yu; but, instead of killing the General, Cao Cao treated Guan Yu with honor before allowing him to return to Liu Bei's service. As a return favor for this kindness, Guan Yu allowed Cao Cao and his men to escape; but that is another story for another time.

Just as Salamis ended the Persian invasion of Greece, the Battle of Red Cliff blocked Cao Cao's southward march. He lost all of his ships and much of his army in the battle. His dream of uniting the realm sank with his invasion fleet to the bottom of the Yangtze River.

In the confusing aftermath of the battle, Liu Bei took control of Jing-Zhou and made it the foundation of his own kingdom.

The Battle of Red Cliff was the basis for the beginning of the storied Romance of Three Kingdoms. In terms of Chinese folklore, it was the equivalent to Homer's Iliad, with the flaming ships playing the role of the wooden horse.

CHAPTER 19. THE BATTLE OF BO-JU, SUN TZU'S SIGNATURE CAMPAIGN

The Battle of Bo-Ju was the culmination of a long campaign fought in 506 BC between Wu and Chu, two major kingdoms of the Spring and Autumn Era.

In 512 BC, He Lu (King of Wu) hired Sun Tzu to train his army. Sun Tzu analyzed the situation and realized the Chu kingdom was too big to chew up in one bite. It was the largest nation of the land, could field a million men under arms, and had many satrapy states under its sway.

Sun Tzu first attacked and conquered the Xu and the Zhong Wu, two of Chu's satraps. King He Lu wanted to ride the victories into the Chu kingdom, but Sun Tzu disagreed. He felt the situation was not yet ripe for an invasion of the Chu. Instead, he divided the Wu army into three units, with each unit taking turns raiding the eastern frontier of the Chu nation.

For six years, the Wu army conducted forays into Chu territory and withdrew each time the Chu army counterattacked. The Wu attacks honed the combat skills of its men, while creating the misconception in the Chu leadership that the Wu army was only interested in spoil attacks on the Chu borders.

In 506 BC, the Chu army attacked its small northern neighbor, the Cai kingdom. Cai sought help from the Wu kingdom. At the same time Cai's neighboring state, the Tang, also had a grudge against the Chu kingdom. Sun Tzu decided it was time to attack the Chu nation.

King He Lu sailed up the Huai River with 30,000 men; then, with guides from the Cai and Tang armies, marched across the land to the east bank of the Han River on the northern border. By advancing on the northern route, the Wu army bypassed the Chu defensive points on its eastern border and circled around into the heartland of the Chu kingdom. It was not unlike Hannibal's march across the Alps to invade Rome.

Alarmed by the Wu invasion, King Zhao of Chu abandoned his attack on Cai and sent an army of 200,000 against the invaders. Nang Wa, the prime minister, led the Chu army with the support of General Shen Yin Shu.

General Shen suggested Nang Wa collect all the boats along the Han River and hold the main army on its west bank, while Shen marched north to Fang-Cheng on the Chus' northern frontier. He would destroy the Wu ships on the Huai River and block the three strategic passes along the Wu army's route of withdrawal. Nang Wa could then cross the Han River, and their two forces would pinch the Wu army from the front and the rear. Nang accepted the plan and Shen departed for Fang-Cheng with 10,000 men.

After Shen's departure, General Wu Cheng Hei of the Chu army suggested the Chu army should attack the enemy immediately to prevent General Shen, a political rival of the Chu Prime Minister, from gaining all the glories of the victor. Nang Wa agreed and launched his attack.

Once across the Han River, the Chu soldiers met a battalion of three hundred Wu soldiers wielding giant long poles and stationed at Xiao Bie Mountains. The Chu troops had never encountered such strange weapons and tactics. The Chu battle line disintegrated under the pummeling by Wu soldiers. After the skirmish, the Wu army withdrew eastward to Bo-Ju, near the Da Bie Mountains.

Nang Wa thought the Wu army would be celebrating their victory and decided to raid the Wu camp that night. However, Sun Tzu had expected the night attack and ambushed the attackers instead. Nang Wa was trounced again, but he was rescued by General Wei She with a reinforcement of 10,000 men.

Nang Wa wanted to repeat the attack with the newly arrived fresh troops, but General Wei disagreed. The disunited Chu army ended up in two camps, five kilometers apart. In the morning, Fu Gai, King He Lu's younger brother, took 5,000 men and attacked Nang Wa's encampment. The Chu army was surprised and routed a third time. Sun Tzu had not been aware of Fu Gai's attack against the enemy but quickly sent in the main force to exploit the situation.

Remnants of Nang Wa's army fled to General Wei She's encampment. The Chu general decided to withdraw to Ying, the capital of the Chu nation; but first, he had to hold off the pursuing Wu army. General Wei deployed his men to defend the beachhead.

To his surprise, the Wu army did not press home its victory. Sun Tzu withdrew his force for ten kilometers and set up camp. The Wu army's failure to follow up on their attack convinced General Wei that the Wu army had no wish for frontal attacks. The General allowed his men to rest and have a meal before initiating the retreat across the Han River.

When a third of the Chu force had embarked aboard ships to cross the river, the Wu army attacked. The panicked Chu army fell apart; soldiers clamored to board their ships to escape from the enemy, and those who could not get aboard fled along the river banks and were slaughtered. General Wei died in the rearguard action. The Wu army pursued them across the Han River and marched toward Ying, the Chu capital. They swept aside the feeble Chu resistance and sacked Ying.

He Lu had defeated the Chu army but could not hold onto his conquest. Shen Bao Xu, a Chu courtier, fled to the Ch'in kingdom and persuaded the King of Ch'in to send an army to evict the Wu invaders. That plus the unexpected incursion by the Yue army into the Wu homeland forced He Lu to take his army and go home.

In the final analysis, if Nang Wa had stuck to General Shen's battle plan, the outcome of the battle might have been different. The internal power struggle within the corrupt Chu court made the kingdom vulnerable to external threats. That is what allowed Sun Tzu to make extensive preparations to weaken the enemy, create misconceptions in the minds of his foes, and choose the time and place of the battle; then he was prepared to take advantage of his enemy's mistakes.

The Battle of Bo Ju was one of the first large-scale military campaigns of the Spring and Autumn Era. Ironically, in 473 BC, only three decades after King He Lu almost conquered the Chu kingdom, the kingdom of Wu itself would be conquered by the rising power of Yue; who in turn would be conquered by the Chu, the initial loser of the Bo-Ju campaign.

CHAPTER 20. THE BATTLE OF ZUI-LI, THE BATTLE THAT SUN TZU LOST

In 506 BC, King He Lu of the Wu kingdom used Sun Tzu to train the Wu army and then led them in a successful campaign against the Chu kingdom in the west. While the Wu army was engaged in fighting the Chu state, King Yun of the Yue nation raided the Wu border, forcing He Lu to abandon his conquest and return home.

In May of 496 BC, King Yun of the Yue kingdom died. King He Lu rejoiced at the demise of his southern nemesis. It was an opportunity not to be wasted. He Lu marshaled his army to punish the Yue Kingdom. Gou Jian, the new ruler of Yue, led his army and met the Wu invaders at Zui-Li.

The Wu army had the advantage of numbers and quality. They were trained and led by the famous General Sun Tzu who had earlier defeated the numerically superior Chu army.

Gou Jian's men charged the Wu army twice and were thrown back both times by the well-disciplined invaders. On the brink of defeat, Gou Jian devised a macabre strategy to disrupt and defeat the enemy.

From the Yue army, seventy-five soldiers were picked to march out in three ranks toward the Wu army. They halted within hailing distance of the Wu position, then the first rank of Yue soldiers shouted in unison, "We are soldiers who have violated military regulations. We are not brave enough in battle but dare not escape our punishment. We are here to commit suicide to atone for our errors." In unison, they drew their swords and slit their own throats. After the first row of Yue soldiers fell to earth, the second rank stepped forward, repeated the same statement as their comrades and then they too committed suicide. By the time the third rank stepped up to emulate the deeds of the previous two ranks, the soldiers of the Wu army had unwittingly moved out of their battle formations and were jostling for a view of the macabre spectacle.

Gou Jian watched as the Wu army dissolved into a disorganized mob of spectators. When the last row of Yue suicide soldiers fell to the ground, Gou Jian sprang his attack. This time, the Wu soldiers were unprepared to counter the Yue assault and were routed. For once, even the brilliant Sun Tzu had to flee from the field.

King He Lu was mortally wounded in the heel during the frantic retreat from battle. On his deathbed, King He Lu ordered his son Fu Chai to avenge his (He Lu's) death.

Historical note: Historical records have revealed conflicting views on whether Sun Tzu was present at the Battle of Zui-Li. One version indicated that Sun-Tzu had retired and left king He Lu after the Bo-Ju campaign. Whatever version held true, the fact was that the army Sun Tzu trained was defeated at Zui-Li by Gou Jian's suicide ploy.

CHAPTER 21. THE PATH OF VENGEANCE

King He Lu of the Wu kingdom received a mortal wound at the Battle of Zui-Li. On his deathbed, he told his son Fu Chai, "Avenge me against the Yue kingdom."

After He Lu's death, Fu Chai became king. He installed an official at the entrance to the palace. Every time Fu Chai walked by, the official would shout aloud, "Fu Chai, have you forgotten that the King of Yue killed your father?"

Fu Chai would cry and respond, "No, and I shall not forget."

In 494 BC, two years after the defeat at Zui-Li, Fu Chai launched his revenge attack against the Yue kingdom. At Gui-Ji, Sun Tzu ordered detachments of Wu soldiers to hold torches and advanced on two flanks toward the Yue army, while the main force attacked from the center. The ploy disheartened the Yue troops; they thought they were facing an overwhelming number of enemies. The Yue army collapsed and King Gou Jian was trapped. He was about to commit suicide, but Minister Wen Zhong stopped him. The Minister said, "Bo Pi, the Wu courtier is avaricious and thus can be bribed. Let me go negotiate a surrender." Gou Jian loaded up Wen Zhong with treasures and then sent him to negotiate for peace with Fu Chai.

Bo Pi was a court favorite of Fu Chai. He took Wen Zhong's gifts and persuaded Fu Chai to accept the surrender from the Yue ruler under the condition that Gou Jian became a slave to Fu Chai. Wu Tze She, the Wu Prime Minister, opposed the surrender. He wanted Gou Jian killed to forestall future problems, but he was overruled by Fu Chai.

Fu Chai withdrew his army and Gou Jian followed with his entourage of courtiers into the Wu kingdom as hostages of the Wu court at Gu-Xu. Gou Jian and his wife were sent to maintain the Wu royal ancestral tombs, including that of King He Lu. They also worked in the royal stable. Whenever the King of Wu rode in a carriage, Gou Jian would be in front leading the horses.

For three years, Gou Jian and his wife worked as obedient and loyal servants to Fu Chai. When Fu Chai was ill, Gou Jian voluntarily tasted the King's feces to diagnose the ailment. Meanwhile, Gou Jian's courtiers piled more treasures on Bo Pi. The courtier also wanted the Yue hostages to be gone, so as to reduce the chance of people learning about his taking bribes from Gou Jian. He convinced the King to let Gou Jian return to the Yue kingdom. Again Prime Minister Wu objected, but to no avail.

Once home, Gou Jian prepared to take back the kingdom. He lived in an austere environment. He slept on a thin layer of straw and hung a gall bladder in his room. Each morning, he would lick the bitter tasting gall to remind himself of the defeat by the Wu kingdom.

48. Gou Jian slept on straw and licked the bitter gall daily to motivate himself to avenge the defeat by Fu Chai.

To encourage production, he personally farmed the land and his wife wove clothing. He set up reward programs to promote population growth. He eliminated taxes for ten years. He forbade older people from marrying younger mates. When a girl reached the age of seventeen or a young man reached twenty and still was not married, his or her parents would be punished. All pregnancies were reported to the local magistrate, who would send a midwife to assist in child delivery. For a baby boy, the family received two jugs of wine and a dog, while a baby girl was rewarded with two jugs of wine and a piglet. On the birth of twins, the government provided extra food and clothing to the family; the government would hire nursemaids for families of triplets.

Gou Jian also routinely sent gifts to Wu courtiers, who in turn shielded the Yue kingdom from the hawkish Wu Tze She. Gou Jian used every means possible to weaken the Wu kingdom. He sent a pair of beautiful women, Xi Shi and Zheng Dan, to Fu Chai as a tribute. The women distracted Fu Chai and the king neglected his royal duties. Gou Jian ordered 3,000 men to cut down tall trees; then had artisans carve intricate designs on the tree trunks before sending them as presents to Fu Chai. Overjoyed by the beautiful beams, Fu Chai commissioned major construction work for his palace.

Gou Jian next arranged a phony war with the Chu kingdom. He sent an army to attack the Chu state and then retreated back across the border while being pursued by the Chu army. The fake fight delighted Fu Chai because the Chu had been the historical enemy of the Wu state. It further diminished Fu Chai's suspicion of a possible Yue revolt against the Wu nation.

In 484 BC, Fu Chai decided to attack the Qi kingdom in the north; Gou Jian sent a contingent of his men to help Fu Chai defeat the Qi army. At the victory celebration, while Wu courtiers congratulated the king, Wu Tze She ranted against the threat posed by the Yue kingdom. In exasperation, Fu Chai sent his sword to the pesky Minister Wu (a royal decree for the Minister to cut his own throat with the sword). Before he committed suicide, Wu Tze She told his aides, "After I am dead, take out my eyes and set them atop the city wall at the Eastern Gate. I want to be able to see Gou Jian come and vanquish the Wu nation."

With Wu Tze She's passing, Sun Tzu, who was a close friend of Wu Tze She, decided to leave the Wu kingdom.

Bo Pi was overjoyed; Wu Tze She's death and Sun Tzu's departure made him the Prime Minister, the most powerful person of the Wu court, next to King Fu Cai.

In 482 BC, Fu Chai took the bulk of the Wu army with him to a summit meeting with the other great powers of the land at Huang-Chi. In his absence, Gou Jian launched his attack against the Wu kingdom. The Wu defenders consisted of the dregs of its army. The vengeful Yue army sacked Gu-Xu, the capital and killed the Wu crown prince who commanded the Wu defense forces. Fu Chai rushed back home with his army but his tired soldiers were soundly trounced by Gou Jian.

In desperation, Fu Chai sent Bo Pi with treasures to negotiate for peace with Gou Jian. The King of Yue realized he still was not yet strong enough to wipe out the Wu army, so he accepted the armistice. But, nine years later, in 473 BC, Gou Jian resumed the attack. After two years of fighting, Fu Chai was cornered. He attempted to negotiate a peaceful surrender with Gou Jian, who contemplated but refused the plea for mercy.

In his last moments, Fu Chai had his men wrap a length of silk sash around his eyes and said, "I am too ashamed to face Wu Tze She," then committed suicide with his own sword.

Bo Pi expected to be well treated by Gou Jian but was disappointed when the King of Yue had the Wu Prime Minister executed. Gou Jian would not accept such a treacherous person in his presence.

Chapter 22. Battle of Jin-Yang, the End of the Spring and Autumn Era

In 471 BC, Gou Jian wiped out the Wu nation. With the newly found prestige and power, Gou Jian attended a summit meeting with the great powers of the land. At that meeting, he was recognized as the leader of the central plains. The declaration of the Yue kingdom as the leading power created problems within the Jin kingdom to the north.

The Jin royal court was dominated by four families — the Zhi, Zhao, Wei and the Han; each with more land and men at arms than the King of Jin. The internal strife between the four clans precipitated the decline of the Jin nation. Zhi Yao, the leader of the Zhi family, was the Senior Minister of the Jin court. He saw the Yue ascendency as an opportunity to whittle down the other three leading families of the Jin nation. He suggested that each of the four families give the king of Jin a city with one hundred *li* of territory and 10,000 families. This would raise the stature of the king, thereby rebuilding the stature of the nation. Of course, as the Senior Minister, Zhi Yao would be in charge of the king's new possessions.

Zhi Yao first declared his willingness to donate the land and the people to the king and then asked Minister Han Hu for an equivalent contribution. The Han were the weakest of the four families. Initially, Han Hu refused the request from Zhi but was persuaded by his staff to give up the land and the people. To refuse would have meant war and destruction by the more powerful Zhi family, whereas, by ceding the land and the people, Zhi Yao's arrogance was built up and this bought time and room to maneuver for the Han family.

Minister Wei Ju was the next victim of Zhi Yao's strong-arm tactics. The head of the Wei clan also did not want to submit to Zhi Yao's demand, but he too decided to bide his time and he acceded to Zhi's demand.

Bolstered by his successful ventures against the two families, Zhi demanded the Zhao clan to produce its share of the tithe to the king; however, Zhao Wu Min, head of the Zhao clan, refused to cooperate.

In 455 BC, Zhi Yao used the authority of the king to summon the armies of the Han and Wei clans to jointly attack the Zhao estate. Zhao Wu Min retreated with his army to the fortified city of Jin-Yang in the basin of the Tai Xing Mountain Range. He had chosen the city for its strong walls and had had the foresight to stockpile war supplies in preparation for the coming war.

The Zhao army sat behind their tall walls and wide moat and greeted the attackers with hails of arrows. The Han and the Wei families were unwilling participants in this venture; their armies made only perfunctory assaults against Jin-Yang. Leaders of those two clans even maintained communications with Zhao Wu Min inside the besieged city.

After two years of siege warfare, Zhi Yao decided to enlist the force of nature. He had his men build a dam on the upper reaches of the Fen River where it flowed past a point northeast of Jin-Yang. At the same time, the attackers dug a canal leading from the river southwest toward the besieged city. When the seasonal rain filled the Fen River, Zhi breached the dam and water followed the course of the canal and inundated Jin-Yang. The flood water reached within six feet of the top of the city wall. Survivors in the city escaped to rooftops and had to cook by hanging cooking pots from rafters.

Zhao Wu Min sent an envoy to the Han and Wei camps. The envoy pointed out the threat posed by Zhi Yao. It was obvious that the Han and Wei clans would be next on the chopping block, after Zhao's collapse. Han Hu and Wei Ju readily agreed to turn the tables against Zhi Yao.

On the appointed night, Wei soldiers attacked Zhi troops guarding the dam. The raiders then breached the levee of the canal to direct the flow of the Fen River toward the Zhi camp. At the same time, Zhao soldiers rode rafts and boats and attacked the Zhi encampment. They were supported by Wei and Han armies on their flanks. Zhi Yao woke up in an inundated camp. His army was crushed and Zhi Yao was taken alive.

Zhao Wu Min followed up the victory at Jin-Yang with attacks against the Zhi estate. Every member of the Zhi family, numbering over two hundred, was put to the sword. Zhao Wu Min took Zhi Yao's head and lacquered it into a drinking vessel.

In the aftermath of the Battle of Jin-Yang, the Zhao, Han and Wei clans divided up the Zhi estate. Since the King of Jin had relied on Zhi Yao to maintain power, his demise also spelled the end of the Jin kingdom. The Zhao, Wei, and Han became sovereign states.

The Battle of Jin-Yang marked the end of the Spring and Autumn Era and the beginning of the Warring States Era. The Five Powers of the Spring and Autumn — Ch'in, Qi, Chu, Jin, and Yan, were transformed to the 'Seven Strongs' of the Warring States Era — Ch'in, Qi, Chu, Yen, Han, Zhao, and Wei. More significantly, the ritualistic chivalrous battles of aristocrats turned into violent warfare that involved hundreds of thousands of men in a single campaign.

Chapter 23. Zheng He, the Admiral

Zheng He (AD 1371–1433), also known as Hajji Mahmud Shamsuddin, was a court eunuch of the Imperial Ming Dynasty (1368–1644), soldier, mariner, explorer, diplomat and fleet admiral. From 1405 to 1433, he commanded seven voyages to Southeast Asia, South Asia, the Middle East, Somalia and the Swahili coast.

Born Ma He, Zheng was of Persian ancestry. The name Ma He was a phonetic translation of the Persian name Mahmud. His family served the Mongolian Yuan dynasty in Yunnan Province of China. In 1381, the ten-year-old Ma He was captured by the Ming army, castrated, then dispatched to serve in the household of Prince Ju Li, a son of Ju Yuan-Zhang, the founder and the First Emperor of the Imperial Ming Dynasty.

Ma He was big, tall, and very intelligent. He benefited from Prince Ju Li's policy of educating his aides. The prince noticed Ma He's physical and mental attributes, and the eunuch became the prince's right-hand man. In 1398, the Ming Emperor died and his grandson became Emperor Jianwen. In the following year, Prince Ju Li, who was also King Yen and Commander of the Yanjing (modern day Beijing) garrison, launched a rebellion and took the throne in 1403 as Emperor Yong Li. Ma He was instrumental in making that coup a success. For this, he was appointed as Courtier of the First Rank, Chief Eunuch of the Imperial Palace, with the title of San Bao Tai Jian (Three Treasure Eunuch), and the Emperor honored him by bestowing on him the name of Zheng He in commemoration of his military achievement at Zheng Cun Ba during the insurrection.

In 1404, Zheng served as envoy to Japan and convinced the King of Japan to quell the pirates that were raiding Chinese coasts. The King arrested the culprits and shipped them to China, where they were steamed to death. The King also submitted as a vassal to the Ming Emperor.

In 1405, Emperor Yong Li sent Zheng He as the Imperial Military Commander of the greatest naval expedition in history to the South China Sea, the Indian Ocean then Africa. Zheng He's fleet departed July 11, 1405, from Suzhou. It was a well-organized expedition with 63 treasure ships and 254 support vessels. On board were almost 28,000 soldiers, sailors, astrologers, Buddhist monks, Daoist priests and support personnel that included ten interpreters/translators.

The fleet consisted of seven types of ships:

Treasure ships (宝船, *Bǎo Chuán*) — They were four-tiered, nine-masted fleet carriers of the time, about 416 feet long and 170 feet wide, used by Zheng He and his deputies as command vessels and for storage of collected valuables. Each ship had the capacity to carry 800 men.

Equine ships (馬船, *Mǎ Chuán*) — They carried horses, tribute goods and repair material for the fleet; eight-masted, about 339 feet long and 138 feet wide.

Supply ships (粮船, *Liáng Chuán*) — As described by their names, these ships carry onboard food and supplies for the crew; seven-masted, 257 feet long and 115 feet wide.

Troop ships (兵船, *Bīng Chuán*) — six-masted, 220 feet long and 83 feet wide.

Fuchuan warships (福船, *Fú Chuán*) — named for their place of origin, Fujian Province; five-masted war junks, up to 165 feet long with a 100-crew capacity.

Patrol ships (坐船, *Zuò Chuán*) — eight-oared, 120 feet long; dinghies for transportation and communications. This type of ships is especially useful in becalmed waters and along shorelines.

Water tankers (水船, *Shuǐ Chuán*) — each ship carried a month's supply of fresh water. These ships were built with individual watertight holds to prevent cross-contamination of spoiled water in other compartments.

It was a diplomatic mission, not an invasion fleet. However, when required, Zheng He did not shy away from the use of force. He ruthlessly suppressed pirates who plagued Chinese and southeast Asian waters. He even brought one of the pirate leaders back to Beijing for execution. He fought a battle against a local kingdom at Ceylon and displayed his military force to intimidate local officials in Arabia and East Africa when they threatened his fleet.

Zheng He visited Brunei, Thailand and Southeast Asia, India, the Horn of Africa, and Arabia. He presented gifts of gold, silver, porcelain, and silk to local kingdoms; in return, he brought back ostriches, zebras, camels, and ivory. Numerous kingdoms he visited sent envoys with Zheng He's fleet to pay homage to the Ming Emperor.

49. Comparison of Zheng He's Treasure Ship and that of Christopher Columbus. A display at the Ibn Battuta Mall in Dubai, UAE.

Over 28 years, Zheng He made seven trips to the South China Sea and Africa. He died in India during the last trip in 1433. To this date, temples, and shrines of Zheng He dotted the landscape of Southeast Asia.

It should be noted that, contrary to popular belief, the main purpose of Zheng He's expeditions was not to expand Chinese power or trade. Prior to 1405, China had no tradition of an oceangoing navy. Emperor Jianwen, the emperor who was overthrown in 1403, had disappeared during the coup. There were rumors that he had escaped to the South Seas. Thus, it was no coincidence that Zheng He started his voyages in 1405 (given time to build the fleet and assemble the manpower), and the abrupt end of naval expeditions within years of the death of Emperor Yong Li. It went down as the greatest manhunt in history.

Chapter 24. Jing Ke, the Death Warrior

Traditionally, senior aristocrats of China maintained a staff of houseguests. They were men of varied talents and served as advisors and henchmen for their lord. The central core group of the houseguests formed the 'Death Warriors' of the aristocrat. Death Warriors did not necessarily deal with death; rather they were willing to die to accomplish their lord's bidding. The lords treated them with extreme respect; in return they offered unquestioning loyalty to their masters. They were one of the most dangerous weapons a lord could use against an enemy. They were the forerunners of the Japanese Ninjas. Jing Ke was one of the most famous Death Warriors of Chinese history.

* * *

In 232 BC, Crown Prince Dan of the Yan kingdom was a courtier at Xian-Yang, capital of the Ch'in kingdom. He was serving as an exchange hostage to ensure friendly relations between the Ch'in and Yan kingdoms. The prince was dismayed at the aggressive intentions of the Ch'in kingdom against other nations. He requested to return home but was refused and ridiculed for his efforts. In desperation, he managed to escape home to the Yan kingdom.

Dan felt the weight of his country's survival on his shoulders as he realized it was only a matter of time before the Ch'in army stormed across the Yi River at the western border of the Yan kingdom. How could they prepare for the oncoming flood? They could strengthen the dams to protect their home; they could dredge the river to divert water away; then they could pray that their ancestors were favored by the gods.

Crown Prince Dan took personal charge of the nation's defenses. Granted, the Yan army was loyal and well-seasoned, but it was lacking in manpower. He needed to strike a careful balance of resources to maintain a viable standing army and work on the defensive infrastructure while leaving sufficient manpower to produce food for the nation. At his insistence, his father the king dispatched emissaries to mend political fences with their neighbors. The diplomatic mission to Lin-Zi would be an especially difficult sell because the crafty and much despised Qi kingdom in the south was the traditional enemy of the Yan nation, but an attempt had to be made.

For over a year, the Yan Crown Prince surveyed the country and inspected every military unit to bolster its military readiness. In the end, he retreated to his palace in utter despair. It was obvious; nothing short of a miracle could save the Yan kingdom from the inevitable Ch'in invasion. The Yan economy simply could not support a standing army of sufficient size to fend off the Ch'in legions. They lacked a large population base to draw recruits from, and time to arm and train them, and lacked an able commander to lead the men to victory. News from the diplomatic front was equally depressing. One after another, Yan emissaries returned to Yi with no alliance agreement from other states.

Xian-Yang had done its work well to prepare its neighbors for conquest. The Ch'in kingdom had vigorously applied the three-hundred-year-old grand strategy — befriend the distant and attack the near. The Ch'in court had diplomatically engaged and made alliances with the nations furthest away from them while its army nibbled away at the neighboring states.

Through bribery, threats, and skullduggery, King Zheng of the Ch'in nation prevented the powerful Qi in the east and the Chu in the south from allying with the other kingdoms. Han, the weakest of Chin's neighbors, had already been annexed into the Ch'in state. The Zhao had yet to recover from the Chang-Ping disaster of thirty years ago and was fast becoming irrelevant. It was doing its best to just survive.

Ironically, while the Ch'in were threatening the western border of the Wei kingdom, the King of Wei decided to pick a fight against the Qi kingdom in the east and suffered a major defeat. Rumor had it that Xian-Yang had goaded the Wei to attack the Qi by promising not to attack them in the meantime.

Distrust, hubris, and fear of Ch'in reprisal precluded a viable military alliance against the Ch'in. In addition, Dan's spies learned that numerous courtiers in many nations had been bought off by Xian-Yang; the few men of integrity that could not be bribed were killed or destroyed by their colleagues who had been compromised by the Ch'in.

Crown Prince Dan felt trapped. He had an army of 200,000 men, but that was less than half of what the Zhao had lost at Chang-Ping. Of course, Zhao Gua was an incompetent idiot, but neither did Dan have a Bai Chi on hand; and there was no reliable ally who could come to their aid in the fight.

There was only one viable solution, a desperate but daring gamble — to assassinate King Zheng. His sudden demise would create a succession crisis which could be exploited. Perhaps the next king would be less aggressive and a surprise attack with 200,000 men at that time would stand a greater chance of success. If nothing else, it could delay the Ch'in expansion and give time for the other kingdoms to build a stronger defense. But, the consequences of a failure would be catastrophic; it would point the Ch'in spear directly at Yi.

Dan sought counsel from his teacher, Chu Wu, who arranged a meeting with Tien Guang, a martial arts master and a man of honor. Prince Dan met Tien at the entrance to the Eastern Palace. The prince personally walked up to the carriage and held the reins for Tien Guang to disembark. In the great hall, Dan symbolically swept the seat cushion at the place of honor with his own sleeve before offering it to Tien Guang. The generous gesture extracted silent gasps and surprised stares from the household staff and resident retainers.

The Yan Crown Prince dismissed his entourage, then sat cross-legged on his own cushion and bowed at the waist to the sage. "Master Tien, you honor us with your presence. I thank you in advance for the great deed you are about to accomplish for your country." He paused to pour tea, then continued when Tien Guang bowed to thank the prince for the tea. "As you are aware, the Ch'in and the Yan are like the fire and the water, it's impossible for them to coexist. I beseech you in the name of the people to save us from annihilation by that tyrant who rules at Xian-Yang.

"I would like you to lead a group of men and assassinate Zheng."

Tien Guang nodded in agreement with the Prince's political assessment, then shook his head. "I am an old war horse that has seen the best of his days. Master Chu remembers me as I was during my youth, but he did not account for the ravages of time."

Prince Dan was grasping at straws and persisted. "Time might have sapped your body of strength, but that has been replaced with knowledge and wisdom. I am counting on your sage advice and experience. You can still lead men and plan an attack, or perhaps you can recommend some younger men who can perform the deed."

The old sage stroked his beard as he pondered the prince's request, then gave an emphatic nod. "Perhaps I can begin by helping you assess the quality of the men you already have in readiness."

Any reservation Prince Dan may have had regarding Tien Guang's qualifications evaporated with the revelation that the old sage was aware of the existence of Dan's small band of assassins. It only validated the man's credentials as a strategist with a wide network of contacts. "Please come with me."

Tien Guang pushed the floor with his right hand and got to his feet with an agility that defied his age.

Dan nodded in approval and gestured with his hand for the old sage to walk ahead of him. Tien Guang in turn waited and gestured for the Prince to take the lead. They walked to the inner courtyard, which looked like an exercise ground with racks of weapons against one wall and heavy stone weights with carved handholds stacked in a corner.

The Prince sent a servant to summon the three assassins he kept in the palace — Hsia Fu, Song Yi, and Ch'in Yang-Wu. As the three men bowed to the Prince, he introduced the warriors to Tien Guang.

Tien Guang surprised the Crown Prince by refusing to acknowledge and return the greetings from the three men. He sent Hsia Fu to fetch tea from the kitchen. Hsia Fu's face turned red with anger at being told to perform a servant's duty. Song Yi's face changed to shades of green when he had to bring water from the well. Chin Wu-Yang's face turned white when Tien Guang merely sneered at the young man and dismissed him with the wave of a hand.

After the assassins had been dismissed, Tien Guang turned to the Prince and said, "Sir, I regret to advise you that none of those men is worthy of your trust and confidence for the intended venture. While they may be valiant fighters, they are also men who easily give way to their emotions.

"I can read their thoughts on their faces. When one is unable to control and disguise one's emotion, one alerts the opposition to the coming attack and thus becomes a threat to the mission." He paused and lifted a palm to forestall a budding protest from the Crown Prince. "However, all is not lost. I have a man who should be suitable to your needs. He is courageous, skilled at martial arts, reliable and in total control of his emotions."

Prince Dan's disconsolate face brightened at Tien Guang's comment. "Who is this person? Where is he from? Is he available? How do I find him?"

"His name is Jing Ke, a descendant of the Jing clan of the Qi nation. His ancestors fled that kingdom to escape political persecution."

"I would like to have the acquaintance of Master Jing; would you do me the honor of an introduction?"

"It shall be done as you request. I know where to find him, and I will send him to you as soon as possible."

Prince Dan personally escorted Tien Guang out of the palace. As the old man prepared to mount the coach, Dan stepped closer and whispered, "This is a matter of extreme sensitivity, please do not speak of it to another person."

The old sage smiled and nodded, "Of course; you can be assured no third person will learn of this discussion." He ordered the driver to steer for home, then sent a servant to summon Jing Ke.

In his study, the old sage dismissed the servants, then turned with a sober countenance toward his guest. "You and I have often lamented at the misfortune of not being recognized for our abilities. I am old and feeble; the body cannot meet the demands of the mind.

"In contrast, you are at your prime. I would like you to have the opportunity I never had; thus, through you, I shall partake in the great venture.

"It appears my premonition about a significant event is correct." The old man paused to look at Jing Ke. A gleam in the younger man's eyes reflected interest at the older man's lead-in. Tien Guang smiled and nodded with approval at Jing Ke's patience and self-control over his own emotion.

The old sage slowly sipped his tea and spat a tea leaf back into the teacup. For his part, Jing Ke sat, composed, and waited for Tien Guang to continue. "As you know, Crown Prince Dan has been working day and night to prepare the kingdom for a Ch'in invasion.

"He wants to cut off the snake's head, to eliminate the threat. It may or may not work. The point is, he is seeking men of martial skills — warriors.

"In spite of my seniority, he still wanted me to take part in the planning and execution of the deed. I declined the offer, due to my old age; however, knowing your desires and capabilities, I recommended you in my place. If you are interested, you should make a trip to the Eastern Palace."

"You have but to speak Master, and I shall obey."

Tien Guang nodded, satisfied that his confidence in the younger man had not been misplaced. "I cannot order you to commit the deed. You yourself must decide whether or not to accept the task."

With an emphatic nod, Jing Ke said, "I'll do it," and exhaled in relief at having made the decision.

Tien Guang nodded and paused to stroke the sword by his side. His face took on a faraway look. "It is said the acts and deeds of an honorable man should never be subject to doubt by others. Today, the Crown Prince confided in me with the plot against the Ch'in. He then counseled me to keep it a secret. He questioned my integrity and dependability.

"Since he had qualms about me, he will also doubt those whom I recommend. I will not have my character placed in doubt. After you leave here, tell the Crown Prince that there shall not be a third person, living, that is witting of his plot against the Ch'in." Tien Guang got to his feet, backed up three steps, then drew his sword and slit his own throat.

Surprised, Jing Ke jumped to his feet but was too late to interrupt the suicide. He opened his mouth to call for help, then stopped. He knelt and kowtowed three times to his mentor and benefactor's corpse. Closing the door behind him, Jing Ke mounted the carriage for the Eastern Palace.

Crown Prince Dan treated Jing Ke in the same manner as he had treated Tien Guang. After Jing Ke had been seated, Prince Dan asked, "Where is Master Tien? Why did he not come with you?"

"Master Tien wished for me to tell you that there shall not be a third person, aside from you and me, who is aware of your plan against King Zheng. My Master kissed his own sword with his throat." Only then did the Crown Prince realize the price of his casual misstatement.

Prince Dan sobbed, "Master Tien died needlessly. I am at fault for being disrespectful and careless with my words."

Regaining his composure, Prince Dan summoned his Chief Steward, "Go to Master Tien Guang's residence and make funeral arrangements with full honors for Master Tien." After the Chief Stewart left, Prince Dan bowed formally to Jing Ke. "Master Tien saw fit to guarantee your reliability with his life. I could do no less in honoring his wishes. Are you willing to undertake this endeavor?"

"I shall strive not to misplace your and Master Tien's trust in me. But, what is it that you really want from the Ch'in?" Jing Ke had decided he needed to hear from the prince the exact goal that he wanted to achieve.

"Zheng has an insatiable appetite for conquest. He will not be content until has all the land under the Heaven within his grasp and all the kings prostrating at his feet. The King of Han has already surrendered his fief and General Wang Jian just won another battle against the Zhao. When Zhao falls, the spears of the Ch'in army will be pointed at us, for the Zhao border our western boundary. We must stop Zheng before his army camps at the gates of Ji."

"In that case, how do you intend to counter this threat? Mobilize the army, or do you have other plans?"

"Against the Ch'in, we are weak and our army is small. Jia, the Crown Prince of Zhao, wants to ally with us; but, I feel it is still not enough to fend off the Ch'in army. The Qi and the Wei have long been cowering under the Ch'in's military might; many of their courtiers are on the Ch'in payroll. Those two kingdoms would not make a move without a blessing from Xian-Yang.

"Then there are the Chu, the largest and richest country of the land, even bigger than the Ch'in; but it also has the most corrupt and worthless court under Heaven. Left to its own devices, it would collapse on itself.

"So, whatever that is to be done to stop the Ch'in, we must do it on our own. What I have in mind is a simple but direct strike. Seize the head and the body will follow.

"I propose to assemble a team of assassins and dispatch them in the guise of emissaries to Xian-Yang. They will bear rich gifts to facilitate access to Zheng. Once they are physically near Zheng, they will kidnap and force him to return all the captured land to the other kingdoms; just as Zhao Mo did to Duke Huan of Qi three hundred years ago.

"If Zheng agrees, then we will have achieved our goal. If he refuses, the assassins will kill him. Zheng's death will throw that country into turmoil, with different factions competing for power. Perhaps, under those conditions, the other kingdoms would unite to destroy the Ch'in.

"If nothing else, we would have more time to build up our defenses. What do you think of the plan?"

Jing Ke paused before making his response. "This is something that will have major consequences, with a lasting effect on the entire kingdom. My Prince, it is easier to kill Zheng than to take him alive for blackmail. Would you consider a straightforward assassination of the tyrant?"

"It's best if Zheng can be taken alive. We would then have an opportunity to demand an orderly return of captured territories.

"Although the death of the tyrant would certainly create a power vacuum in Xian-Yang, it does not guarantee the return of the lost land. In fact, a new king would probably emerge before we could get the other powers to join in attacking the Ch'in. Besides, assassins would surely die with Zheng. If Zheng is taken hostage to barter for the land, there is a possibility for you to enjoy the rewards of your labor." Dan did not mention his other reason for not wanting Zheng killed — 'A king should only be killed by another king.' There was no need to encourage regicide by commoners.

Royal builders constructed a brand new mansion just for Master Jing. Legions of servants and slaves ensured he lacked for nothing. A bevy of beauties alleviated his ennui. Silk robes, chauffeured carriages, and other fineries educated Jing Ke about the cultured life of an aristocrat.

Each day, the future ruler of the realm visited his newfound friend. One day, the Prince took Master Jing on a tour of the Eastern Palace. A turtle emerged on the surface of a fishpond to greet the visitors. Jing Ke picked up some pebbles to throw at the reptile. When he had finished tossing the pebbles, he turned and found Prince Dan standing next to him holding a bowl of gold nuggets for young Master Jing to use on the turtle.

The crown prince, an avid equestrian, often took Master Jing on riding excursions. On the day the builders completed construction of the new mansion, Jing Ke again rode at the side of Crown Prince Dan. In fine spirit, the prince easily won an impromptu race against Jing Ke. As they walked the horses to cool them off, Jing Ke commented on the quality of the prince's mount. Dan proudly recounted the lineage of his prize steed, and added, "its name is 'Wind Chaser.' It cost one thousand taels of gold, and I have already won more than that amount in wagers against other lords and dukes of the realm."

In a moment of jovial levity, Jing Ke jested, "Did you know that the liver of a fine stallion is one of the best delicacies to accompany fine wine?" That evening, at the banquet given in his honor, a servant set down a dish of dark reddish-brown flesh in front of Jing Ke. Rising curls of steam indicated it was a fresh kill. An almost imperceptible nod from the host to Jing Ke confirmed it was The Wind Chaser's liver. Tears of shame and gratitude glistened in Jing Ke's eyes, as he lifted the wine cup to thank his host, then sampled a piece of the gift. Jing Ke vowed to be more selective in the choice of his words when conversing with his benefactor.

A month later, in the privacy of Prince Dan's study, Jing Ke presented a general outline of the attack plan. "King Zheng is a survivor and not a trusting person. He has lived in spite of numerous attempts against his life. He distrusts everyone. No one, including his royal guardsmen, are allowed to be near him with a weapon, without his personal authorization. And nobody, not even the Chief Steward of the Palace, knows where the king beds down each night.

"As I see it, our preparations must be accomplished in stages. First, we need lures of sufficient value to entice Zheng into admitting the assassination team into his court. If we can't get into the royal court, we will not be able to accomplish our mission.

"Next, we need a suitable weapon or weapons for the task. For that, I'd suggest a sharp dagger treated with a poisonous solution. A dagger is easier to conceal, and poison will induce death at the slightest wound.

"Lastly, we need a way to smuggle the weapon into the Ch'in court; everyone and everything is searched prior to entering that palace. The doors to the palace entrances are made of magnetic rock to detect metallic weapon.

"I'd also like to point out that it would be difficult enough to kill Zheng but to take him alive and force him to negotiate the return of the captured territories would be nigh on impossible. So, if we are to assume this venture, we should start with the premise of killing King Zheng as our goal. Otherwise, it will be an exercise in futility."

"Alright," Prince Dan nodded, "I agree with your assessment. What do you have in mind for gaining entry into the Ch'in court?"

"We start by offering Du Keng to Zheng, the richest territory of this nation, which feeds on the tyrant's weakness for territories. The assassination team will bring the map of the territory as a tribute, under the pretext of recognizing the Ch'in as the sovereign power. Zheng will want to see the map, providing the opening for the assassins to get near him. The weapon would be hidden in the rolled up map scroll.

"I would like to meet other members of your assassination team; especially General Fan Yu-Chi, the man whose head is worth 10,000 pieces of gold. He may provide some insight into Zheng's habits that may be of value to our plans."

"Good idea. I shall invite the men to dinner tomorrow night."

Next evening, General Fan and the other men arrived in carriages for the dinner banquet. As usual, Jing Ke sat at the seat of honor, with the host and General Fan on either side of him. The three assassins, Hsia Fu, Song Yi and Chin Wu-Yang rounded out the guest list.

Prince Dan recounted, for the amusement of his guests, the tales of his flight back home from Xiang-Yang. Halfway into Dan's story, his newest favorite courtesan showed up to serve wine to the guests. She then played the gu-zheng, the thirteen-stringed musical instrument, to entertain the guests. Jing Ke closed his eyes and lost himself to the crisp floating notes. When he opened his eyes, he saw nothing but two pearl white hands, with long delicate fingers dancing over the frets. Jing Ke admired the beauty of the woman and her talented skill, and could not help to comment wistfully, "What a pair of exquisite and talented hands."

At the end of the festivities, Prince Dan summoned carriages to take his guests home. As Jing Ke mounted his carriage, the Prince signaled for a servant to come forward with a lacquered box. "A small memento as a symbol of my respect for your person."

In the privacy of his room, Jing Ke opened the gift box from the prince. Under the wavering candlelight, a pair of pearl white hands rested on a bed of black silk cloth. The contrasting colors accentuated the frail beauty of the ghoulish present. Jing Ke solemnly buried the lacquered box, along with its contents, at a small knoll in the garden of his mansion. He offered a prayer for the owner of the hands and vowed to recompense the Crown Prince for his generosity and attentiveness.

A month later, in one early morning, Jing Ke completed a set of exercises in the garden. He paused to wipe off his sweat and noticed a servant waiting under the moon gate at the garden entrance. Jing Ke nodded for the man to approach.

He bowed and announced, "Master, the Crown Prince is here to see you."

Jing Ke hurried to pull on his robe, "Why didn't you tell me earlier?"

"I dare not Master; His Highness forbade me to interrupt your morning exercise. He said he would wait for you in the study."

Jing Ke rushed into his study and found the Yan Crown Prince sipping tea at a low table. Crown Prince Dan's tightly creased brows hinted at the presence of a major crisis. "Your Highness, your disposition is disquieting. Is there a problem?"

The prince dispensed with the formalities and went to the point. "Master Jing, there has been distressing news from the west. Time runs short for us to act against the Ch'in. General Wang Jian had just taken Han-Dan, and the King of Zhao surrendered the kingdom to General Wang. Our western border now abuts that of the Ch'in.

"I have already mobilized the army, increased the border patrols and redoubled the war preparation efforts.

"I believe now is the time to finalize the details of our plan against Zheng. It will not be long before the Ch'in army crosses the Yi River to attack us."

"Your Highness, I have thought about the problem and, based on our previous discussions, I came up with a plan for your approval. We start with offering Du Keng to gain entry into the Xian-Yang court. We still need a poison-laced dagger. Finally, I sent for Master Guy Nieh, the best swordsman under Heaven; with him on our team, the chance of success more than doubles. He is a citizen of the Zhao kingdom and thus would agree to join us in our effort.

"I met him before, when I tried to join his martial arts school, but he refused to accept me as a student. But I think he will join us to save his nation."

Prince Dan nodded, "I think we need more than the map of Du Keng to get into the Ch'in court. Ch'in has grown into a large country; the offering of an additional piece of land may not pique his interest sufficiently to get the team in. However, the map does serve the purpose of transporting the weapon into the Chin court."

Jing Ke slowly turned the teacup in his palm, as he thought over the problem. At length, he lifted his head to look at the Prince. "The only other item in your possession that might be of interest to Zheng is General Fan."

Prince Dan's eyes widened with incredulity at Jing Ke's words. The Yan Crown Prince shook his head emphatically, "No, no, no! You cannot expect me to give up General Fan. He came to me at his time of need. I will not betray the trust of a friend." Jing Ke nodded his submission to the Prince's decision and dropped the subject.

After Prince Dan departed, Jing Ke summoned his carriage and headed for General Fan's residence. Fan Yu Qi received his guest in the study. "Master Jing, what fine wind brought you to my humble abode? How may I be of assistance to you?"

"Zheng's army has just conquered Han-Dan and taken the King of Zhao prisoner." Jing Ke paused for General Fan Yu-Qi to absorb the news. "My friend, you have suffered much at the hands of that tyrant; your parents, family, and clansmen, all massacred by Zheng's order. He even ransomed your head for 10,000 taels of gold. Now that he has conquered Zhao, he will be coming to Yan to hunt you down. Your presence here has guaranteed the arrival of the Ch'in army. What are you going to do?"

The general lifted his face as tears streamed down his cheeks. "Every night, I have thought of my family and the man responsible for their deaths. The only reason that I am still alive is to seek revenge against Zheng. I will gladly die if only I can take Zheng with me."

"Would you be willing to participate in a daring venture? Its success will rid the Yan kingdom of its threat and, at the same time, avenge your family's death."

"What is this plan?" Jing Ke hesitated, which prompted General Fan to prod him. "Master Jing, why do you not speak?"

"I have a plan; but, it is difficult to put into words."

"If you have a plan that can rescue Yan and avenge my family, I want to hear about it. I will gladly do anything to make your plan come to fruition. Why is it so difficult to tell me about it?"

"My plan is actually very simple. I plan to assassinate Zheng, and I require a means to get near him. If you would loan me your head, as a present to Zheng, he will surely see me. When I get near him, I will grab him with my left hand and use my right hand to bury a dagger in his chest. This way, your family and you would be avenged, and Yan will be saved from conquest. That is my plan."

General Fan sat up erect then bowed deeply to Jing Ke, "Master Jing, I and my clan thank you in advance for planning and executing this fine plan. You have solved my problem for me. I can now go in peace to meet my ancestors. Please convey my appreciation and gratitude to the Prince for his kind hospitality." With those words, General Fan stood up and bowed to Jing Ke again. "And, please accept this bow as my personal acknowledgment of the daring deed you are about to perform. We both know the chance of your survival is nearly nonexistent; however, if your attempt turns out, we shall toast each other again at the Yellow Spring [in the after-life]." Fan Yu Qi then drew his sword and slit his own throat.

"Please wait for me, my friend. We shall meet again at the Yellow Spring." Jing Ke bowed three times to General Fan's corpse, then used General Fan's sword to sever his head from the body.

Jing Ke tore the sleeve off of his own robe, then dipped a finger into the dead man's blood and wrote on the torn sleeve, 'General Fan has donated his head as an instrument to aid in Your Highness' endeavor.' He rolled the sleeve into a scroll, then walked out of the room and summoned a servant, saying, "Take this scroll to the Crown Prince, immediately."

Prince Dan raced to General Fan's residence to grieve and pay respect to a brave friend. He ordered a wooden head be carved for the corpse, so the body could be whole for burial. The severed head, preserved in salt, rested in an ornate cedar box.

While the servants prepared General Fan's body for burial, Jing Ke walked with the Prince in the garden. "Your Highness, please compose yourself. Do not grieve for General Fan; I explained the plan to him and he willingly agreed to his role in the scheme. Now, we must do our part to carry out our plan so that the General will not have died in vain. Do you have a poisoned dagger ready?"

Jing Ke's question awakened Dan to his responsibility and the cause of his friend's suicide. "Thank you, Master Jing, for reminding me of my duty, and the purpose of General Fan's death. I have acquired a two-foot-long sharp blade and had it treated with a poisonous solution. It was tested with a slight cut on a condemned criminal and it caused the man's instant death. Now that we have the necessary equipment, when will you set off for Xian-Yang?"

"I would like to wait for Master Guy Nieh, the sword master I mentioned before. I sent a man to find him, but he was not home. He was a good friend of Master Tien Guang, and I have seen him use a sword to kill a bird in flight.

"What with the Ch'in conquest of the Zhao kingdom, Guy Nieh was probably in hiding from the Ch'in army. We need him to ensure the success of our plan."

"The bow is bent and the arrow is ready to be shot. We cannot wait forever for Master Guy. Besides, we don't know if he would agree to participate in the plan, not to mention the additional security risk in his involvement. The Ch'in army may soon be on the march. Time is of the essence. As for your need of an assistant, you have met my stable of fighting men. I believe the best one is Chin Wu-Yang. He is the youngest and the strongest, and has had experience in the business of killing."

"Your Highness, this undertaking is fraught with difficulties. We are pitting a short blade against the military might of the Ch'in Empire. The probability of success is not high. A swordsman of Guy Nieh's caliber would greatly increase the chances of a success. I am not afraid to die, but I do want our task to succeed. I believe we should use every advantage we could get." He paused to gauge Dan's reaction.

The Prince's mind, already burdened with the pressure of the expected Ch'in threat, collapsed under the combined news of the Zhao kingdom's demise and the sudden suicide of General Fan. His body shook, the mouth opened, but no word came out.

Jing Ke sighed, "Alright, we will do as you say; but, we still need to make one more preparation before we can go to Xian-Yang.

"We need to line the edges and corners of the map box with decorative iron work and do the same to the sandalwood box containing General Fan's head. The metal will disguise the presence of the dagger hidden in the map scroll for inspection at the palace gate at Xian-Yang.

"The work on the boxes will also allow some time to wait for Guy Nieh. If he does not arrive by the time the metal work is done, I shall take Chin Wu-Yang with me. We also need official documents to support our diplomatic status."

Three days later, early in the morning, the Yan Crown Prince led a procession of carriages to the east bank of the Yi River. Everyone wore white, in mourning for Jing Ke and Chin Wu-Yang. Whether they succeeded or failed, this would probably be the last time Prince Dan would see them on this plane of existence. The Chief Steward and a platoon of servants had arrived earlier and set up tents for sacrificial offerings to the gods. The prince led the prayer to the heavenly gods, the earth deities and the ancestral forefathers. He then used the ceremonial wine to toast Jing Ke and Chin Wu-Yang for one last time. Jing Ke accepted and returned toasts from Dan and the other guests.

Gao Jian Li took out his zhu, a kind of zither or dulcimer, and struck the cords. As the notes danced off the fret, Jing Ke stood up from his seat cushion and walked over to the musician. In sync with Gao Jian Li's beat, Jing Ke sang in his deep metallic voice:

> "Oh, the brisk wind blows and the cold Yi River flows;
> Warriors pass onward like the wind and the water."

As the final note faded into the wind, Jing Ke tossed off the last cup of wine, then led the way to his carriage. Prince Dan and his entourage knelt and bowed to Jing Ke and Chin Wu-Yang as they drove their carriage across the bridge toward Xian-Yang and destiny.

Jing Ke registered at an inn and then dispatched a servant with a letter to request a meeting with Meng Jia, a greedy courtier who was also a favorite of King Zheng. Next day, Jing Ke arrived at the Meng residence bearing gifts of gold and jewelry.

The Meng clan has been a powerful family in Xian-Yang for generations, with many of its sons serving in senior military and civil posts in the Ch'in court.

Meng Jia salivated at the unexpected windfall. His eyes squinted into a gleeful thin line as he forced himself to turn away from the glittering baubles. Etiquette demanded a proper response. "To what do I owe this pleasure? I cannot accept such gifts without earning it." The courtier fawned at his guests.

"My Lord, I am Jing Ke, an envoy of the Yan kingdom. My master, Crown Prince Dan, sent me to petition for eternal peace between our two lands. This is but a small token of appreciation for your assistance in the matter."

"Yes, I do recall your crown prince. He did host some most memorable parties. What exactly do you wish for me to do for you?"

"My master and I would be eternally grateful if you would sponsor my entry into King Zheng's court. I bear official documents of the Yan kingdom." Jing Ke reached into his sleeve and brought out a scroll given to him by Dan. It appointed Jing Ke as the official representative of the kingdom. While Meng Jia read the scroll, Jing Ke added, "As a sign of our sincerity, I bring gifts for the King, a map of the Du Keng area, the richest region of our nation; and the head of Fan Yu Chi, the fugitive from your land."

Meng Jia felt his heart pounding faster as he thought of the glory and the additional riches that had just fallen into his clutches. "Where is that traitor's head? Did you bring it with you? It is worth 10,000 taels of gold and the fief of a lordship."

"My master had instructed that I personally deliver the royal gifts to King Zheng." Jing Ke concealed his disgust at Meng Jia's boundless avarice and obvious disappointment. "Would you sponsor my audience with the King?"

With another quick glance at the bundle of gold and jewelry, Meng Jia bobbed his head in quick assent. "Leave your name and that of your hostel with my Chief Steward. I will let you know the date and time of the appointment." Jing Ke bowed his farewell and returned to the hostel.

Next day, near the end of the morning audience, Meng Jia rose from his seat cushion in the royal court and stepped forward to present his supplication. "Master, the gods have seen fit to bestow another favor on your realm. The might of your valiant army has struck such fear into the heart of your foes that it is now capable of winning victories without doing battle." He paused for effect, as the King and members of the court gave the speaker their full attention. "The Yan kingdom has become so terrified of your army that it has dispatched an envoy to beg for mercy.

"The King of Yan offers to submit under your enlightened majesty, and requests only that he remain as ruler of his own land, subordinate to Xian-Yang of course. As a gesture of his allegiance, he has sent you the map of Du Keng and the head of the fugitive Fan Yu Chi. I beseech you to grant an audience to Jing Ke, the Yan envoy."

Silence descended upon the court as it absorbed the surprising news, a silence that was broken when Zheng lifted his head and the great hall echoed with his howling laughter.

Jing Ke and Chin Wu-Yang submitted to body searches for weapons before they were allowed to mount the carriage. Jing Ke carried the box containing Fan Yu Chi's head, while Chin Wu-Yang brought the map container.

As the procession got underway, Jing Ke felt the heavy weight of the wooden box and remembered the bloody price already paid in preparation for this mission — Tien Guang, Fan Yu Chi, the courtesan with the beautiful hands, and Wind Chaser. A man should live a meaningful life and be willing to die for his true friends; Prince Dan, Tien Guang and Fan Yu Qi were indeed true friends. They had given their all to prepare for this day. 'Jing Ke, it is time to prove you are worthy of their friendship; afterward, eternal glory awaits,' he thought to himself.

While Jing Ke found internal peace with his destiny, Chin Wu-Yang could not help but stare at the forest of shiny halberds surrounding his carriage. It was one thing to face an enemy in mortal combat with the outcome in doubt, but quite another to march into certain death.

At the palace entrance, a battalion of ceremonial guards in shiny black armor stood in formation to welcome the Yan envoys. Sensing the discomfort of his assistant, Jing Ke gave the younger man a reassuring smile, then dismounted from the carriage.

As Jing Ke entered the palace, his hand involuntarily swung toward the doorjamb, and the vigilant guards immediately stopped the procession. The guard commander investigated the cause of the blockage. Jing Ke feigned ignorance while guards inspected his arms, robe and finally the iron-filigreed box.

The metallic decorations on the corners of the box appeared to have caused the box to be pulled toward the magnetic door frame. A guard flipped the box top open and was greeted by a grisly severed head within. He grimaced and snapped the box shut, then waved Jing Ke through the gateway.

Chin Wu-Yang followed Jing Ke to the palace gate. This time, when the map box reacted to the magnetic door frame, the guard commander just glanced at the shiny filigree on the box and waved for them to continue into the royal court.

Inside the royal court, the Ch'in courtiers, in full regalia, stood four ranks deep on each side of the center aisle to welcome the newest subjects of their mighty empire. King Zheng smiled with arrogant satisfaction as the Yan envoys entered the great hall.

Ch'in Wu-Yang had experience in killing people but lacked the maturity and fortitude that came with age. The massive martial display and the grandiose dimensions of the Ch'in palace shook the younger assassin's self-confidence. It was one thing to kill a person in a fit of anger and quite another to calmly face certain death against overwhelming odds.

At the intimidating sight of the King, the last remaining vestige of the young man's nerves vanished. His knees weakened, unable to take another step forward, and giant beads of sweat broke out on his forehead. Several courtiers snickered at the obvious timidity of the Yan diplomat, which only further terrified and embarrassed the young assassin.

Too late, Jing Ke realized Ch'in Wu-Yang was too young and inexperienced for the dangerous mission. What was needed was a man like Tien Guang or Guy Nieh, who could stand unflinching in the face of crumbling mountains. Alas, it was too late now to rue his own misjudgment; the only thing to do was to continue with the task.

King Zheng frowned at the cowardly, inappropriate behavior of an official diplomat. It was an insult to dispatch untrained and uncultured men on a diplomatic mission.

Jing Ke, afraid that Zheng might summon a servant to take possession of Ch'in Wu-Yang's map, boldly strode forward and bowed to the king. "Great King, please forgive the failings of a country peasant. He has never encountered a person of your esteemed stature and is obviously intimidated by your august presence. Please forgive him and allow me the honor of completing his mission."

Zheng nodded approval at the eloquence of the senior diplomat from Yan. He snorted and gestured with his jade scepter toward Ch'in Wu-Yang, while he spoke to Jing Ke. "Leave him there. You can bring the map to me." Breathing a sigh of relief, Jing Ke bowed, then knelt to set the wooden box on the edge of the dais. He flipped opened the box to reveal the ash white, severed head of Fan Yu Qi, then spun the container so that the King could see the dead General's face.

King Zheng waved his scepter toward a eunuch, who walked over and lifted the head out of the box by its hair knot and placed it on a silver tray. He brought the tray to the King, knelt to his knees, then raised the tray over his head for inspection. The Monarch regarded the final remains of his hated enemy, then turned to look at Jing Ke. "Why did it take so long for you to bring me the head of the traitor?"

"Great King, the outlaw Fan Yu-Qi had fled to the northern mountains. My master placed the ransom of a thousand pieces of gold on Fan before we were able to capture him. Prince Dan feared that Fan's friends might attempt a rescue, so my master had him executed, then ordered me to bring his head to you." Jing Ke bowed, then backed his way toward Ch'in Wu-Yang; taking the map box out of the immobilized young man's hands, he returned to the dais.

Jing Ke approached the dais with the map. "My king, here is the second gift sent by my master; a map depicting the richest territory of our kingdom." King Zheng waved for the eunuch to remove the tray that held the severed head to make room on the dais. Jing Ke brought the silk scroll out of the box, placed it on the tiled floor of the dais, then sat down and bowed, inviting the King to review the map.

Zheng rose from his seat cushion and walked over to join the Yan envoy. Jing Ke leaned forward and held down the right end of the scroll, then slowly unrolled the map with his left hand. He intentionally shook the map slightly, inducing the King to reach down with his left hand to steady the map. As King Zheng's attention focused on the map of his newly gained territory, Jing Ke unrolled the rest of the map.

The moment the dagger appeared at the end of the scroll, Jing Ke grabbed the weapon with his right hand; at the same time, his left hand reached for the tyrant's arm. The glint of the blade caused the King to flinch. His sudden movement saved him from Jing Ke's grasp. Instead, the assassin only got a hold of the King's sleeve. Jing Ke yanked while Zheng pulled, and the sleeve tore at the shoulder seam just as Jing Ke swung the blade at the king's chest, leaving Jing Ke to stumble back with a fist full of silk sleeve.

He tossed the silk cloth aside, leaped to his feet and went after his quarry. The king scurried behind a large pillar for safety. Pandemonium broke out in the court as Jing Ke chased King Zheng around the pillar.

Ironically, Zheng's own edict worked against him and gave Jing Ke a chance to kill him. The well-disciplined palace guards had specific orders not to enter the royal court without their king's personal authorization, especially not with weapons.

Zheng frantically circled the giant columns, keeping just a step ahead of the assassin's sharp dagger. Temporarily, the King succeeded in evading death, but the need for speed hampered him from drawing his own weapon. The sword at his side measured five feet and, while running for his life, he could only pull the weapon halfway out of the scabbard. His frantic, fumbling fingers did not help the matter. Zheng could not draw the blade without slowing his pace, and to tarry meant certain death.

Zhao Gao, a minor eunuch, noticed Zheng's problem in drawing the sword; the eunuch shouted, "My King, hitch the sword up onto your back, you can draw the sword easier that way."

Xia Wu-Chi, the royal physician, flung his medical box at the assassin. The box took Jing Ke by surprise and caused him to trip and fall; it gave

Zheng the opening he needed to shift the sword at his side onto his back and he drew it out of the scabbard.

The King of Ch'in went on the offensive. His long reach with the sword had an immediate telling effect. Jing Ke leaped backward to dodge a stroke by the King and unexpectedly, his back smashed against a pillar. Before he could recover from the shock, Zheng took a step forward and swung. The sword chopped into Jing Ke's left leg. He fell back against the pillar and slid to the floor. Zheng back away from the wounded assassin, trembling from the close call with death.

Jing Ke took a deep breath and threw the dagger at Zheng. The aim was slightly off, and the blade flew past the king's head and buried itself, to the hilt, into a pillar.

Jing Ke cried out in frustration at the failure of his last ditch effort. He realized that it meant his own death, the failure of his mission, and the wasted deaths of his friends.

He made one more futile attempt to shield Dan and the Yan kingdom. The assassin propped himself against the pillar and laughed. "The only reason that you are still alive is that I did not intend to kill you. My goal was only to force you to return the territories you captured from the other kingdoms. That order from Crown Prince Dan was the only reason that I did not kill you when I first got close to you."

Zheng laughed hysterically at the close call. Not willing to place himself in any more danger, he roared, "Guards, come to me. I command you." The waiting palace guards swarmed into the court and butchered the hapless Ch'in Wu-Yang. Jing Ke did not have long to wait, as a dozen guards raced to be the first at the kill and gain reward from their king.

The King averted his eyes from the slashed face and minced body, as his heart continued racing in his chest. Of all the attempts on his life, that was the closest to success. He waved at the guards and gestured for them to remove the corpses.

As soon as order had been restored, the court waited for King Zheng to unleash his fury, and they were not disappointed. "Every individual involved in this plot will pay for his complicity. I want the heads of the two assassins and that of the rebel Fan Yu Qi dangling at the palace gate.

"Ambassadorial delegations are protected by diplomatic convention; however, these assassins came cloaked in the guise of a diplomatic mission; they have declared war on us. Every member of the Yan delegation is to be rounded up and beheaded."

The greedy Meng Jia bowed his head and started trembling, as he heard his name mentioned by his king. "Meng Jia, you were negligent in exposing your king to danger. By sponsoring the assassins into the court, you are guilty of treason. You are stripped of your rank and you shall suffer the death of 10,000 cuts. Your entire family is sentenced to death and your properties are confiscated."

Meng Jia gave a low moan and collapsed to the floor at the severe sentence.

While palace guards arrived to remove corpses and the prisoner, King Zheng turned to face the royal physician. "Xia Wu Chi, your quick thinking and fast action prevented the assassins from achieving their goal. You shall receive 200 cattys of gold for your devotion and your valuable service to the realm.

"Zhao Gao, you are awarded 100 cattys of gold and promoted to Senior Eunuch. The rest of the courtiers who have been injured in my defense shall also be promoted one rank." Zhao Kao, the royal physician, and the courtiers bowed in appreciation for their rewards.

Within a year, the Ch'in army crossed the Yi River and easily swept the Yan army from the field. King Si, Prince Dan's father, presented his son's head to the Ch'in commander in exchange for an armistice. However, in the following year, another Ch'in army returned and completed the conquest of the Yan kingdom.

50. Chinese commemorative postage stamp depicting Jing Ke's assassination attempt on Qin Shi Huang Di, the First Emperor. The dagger used in the assassination attempt is seen stuck in the pillar. The original print is a stone rubbing from the 3rd century Eastern Han Dynasty.

When news of the failed assassination attempt reached Yu-Ci, Sword Master Guy Nieh summoned his students for a demonstration. He repeated the performance of striking a bird in flight, then broke the sword in two. To the shocked audience, Guy Nieh lamented, "What good are these eyes if they could not recognize the true heart of a man. Jing Ke would have succeeded in his task if only he'd had the benefit of my training." The great sword master reversed the broken blade and cut out his own eyes.

CHAPTER 25. MO DAO, THE FORERUNNER OF THE SAMURAI SWORD

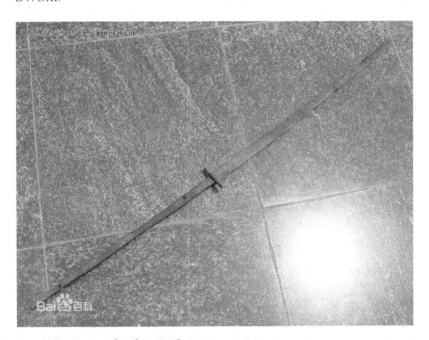

51. Mo Dao artifact from Baidu.com

The Mo Dao was a close combat infantry weapon, not well-known but effective, of the imperial army during the Tang dynasty (AD 618–907) in China. Elite shock troops armed with the Mo Dao shattered enemy formations; they were especially effective in combating nomadic cavalry charges. In the attack, Mo Dao battalions were referred to as meat grinders, scattering enemy flesh and blood across the battlefield. However, the difficult manufacturing process, the exorbitant cost to produce the weapon and the extensive training requirements necessary for its use resulted in its eventual demise and disappearance from the Chinese armory. Due to its lethality and high production cost, the imperial government forbade private ownership of the Mo Dao, which explains why few actual artifacts of the weapon have come to light.

The Mo Dao evolved from the Zhan Ma Dao — 'The Horse Slayer Knife,' of the Imperial Han dynasty (202 BC–AD 220). It was specifically designed for use by the infantry against the cavalry. It was considered a knife because the Chinese categorized single-edged blades as knives; swords were doubled edged.

52. Zhan Ma Dao

The Zhan Ma Dao had the nickname of 'The Three Heads Knife.' Legend had it that with one swing of the blade, one warrior lopped off the heads of a horse, a lance and the opponent at the same time.

The original Zhan Ma Dao was about four feet long, single-edged, had a slightly curved sword blade and a handle that accounted for almost half the length of the weapon. Armorers of the Tang era lengthened it to create an eight-foot long, heavy duty, double-edged straight sword that weighed around 25 pounds. It shared some characteristics with the Scottish claymore; however, the Chinese weapon was longer, thinner, very heavy, and had an extended haft. The extreme length, slender shape, and hefty weight of the weapon allowed the user to wield it like an ax, sword or lance. The abnormal length and weight of the Mo Dao demanded that the user have extraordinary strength and stamina, plus extensive training and practice.

Under the command of a "Mo Dao General," battalions of soldiers armed with the Mo Dao were deployed as shock troops to demoralize and destroy the enemy. Mo Dao troopers were also trained in crossbows and recurve bows. The Tang Imperial military doctrine dictated that crossbowmen fire their weapons when the enemy closed to one hundred and fifty paces; then the recurve bows were fired at sixty paces. When the enemy was within twenty paces, soldiers fired one last missile, then drew the Mo Dao for close combat. The outsized physical stature of the men and their weapons made them natural choices as Imperial Guardsmen for the Emperor; thus the Mo Dao became a status symbol in the society of the Tang Dynasty.

53. Mural of Imperial Guardsman copied from the Tomb of Princess Chang Leh of the Tang Dynasty, Xi'an Museum, Shaanxi Province, China. Note the long Mo Dao, almost twice the length of the shorter standard sword, and the right hand resting over the bow case.

54. Murals of Imperial Tang infantrymen of the Mo Dao Battalion, Tomb of Princess Chang Leh of the Tang Dynasty, Xi'an Museum, Shaanxi Province, China.

The Mo Dao was eventually replaced by the pole ax and halberd, which were cheaper to produce and so could be manufactured in quantity; and they were easier to use. However, thanks to Japanese emissaries, descendants of the Mo Dao survived and proliferated in Japan.

Historical records show that early versions of the Japanese samurai swords were called *Chokuto*, literally translated to 'Knife of the Middle Kingdom,' or 'Knife of China.' It was no coincidence that the first Japanese samurai sword appeared in Japanese annals around AD 700, at the height of the Imperial Tang Dynasty.

During the Tang Dynasty, Japanese rulers routinely sent diplomatic envoys numbering in the hundreds to Chang-An (near modern day Xi-An), the capital of the Imperial Tang Empire. They attended imperial colleges and brought Chinese culture, religion, and technical expertise, to include metallurgy and weaponry, back with them to Japan, thus giving birth to the samurai sword. The Chinese name for the samurai sword is *Wu Shi Dao* (Warrior Knife) due to its single-edge design.

Next to the Katana, the closest weapon to the Mo Dao would be the Scottish claymore which was used to cut down English mounted, armored knights. Both weapons were specially developed for infantry against the cavalry.

CHAPTER 26. CHINESE CROSSBOWS

The crossbow served as an effective force multiplier in ancient times. Unlike the longbow or the recurve bow, the crossbowman required little training to achieve proficiency. A peasant farmer could easily be turned into a competent crossbowman within a ten-day period.

An ancient text from China's Shang Dynasty (1600–1046 BC) describes the crossbow as a mechanical bow. It evolved from the slingshot, a common hunting weapon of the time. The slingshot in Chinese is *Dan Gong* (弹弓), literally, 'the bow that fires round shots.' For comparison, note that another 2,000 plus years transpired before the crossbow made its debut on the battlefields of medieval Europe.

To facilitate mass production of the crossbow, Chinese armorers used standardized crossbow dimensions and introduced mold-cast metal firing mechanisms, identical and therefore interchangeable, to make it possible to use an assembly line to manufacture the weapon. This also facilitated rapid field maintenance of the weapons. The early crossbow even had a notched device on the stock called *Wang Shan* or Watch Mountain to help aim the weapon.

During the Han Dynasty (206 BC to AD 220), crossbows were classified into 1, 3, 4, 5, 6, 7, 8 and 10 stone-weights (*Dan* 石) in terms of strength. One stone-weight was equal to about 30 pounds.

The ten-stone crossbow could cover a range up to 400 meters. The more powerful crossbows came with a stirrup-like handle to carry it by and for use when arming it. A soldier would step on the handle, then pull the bow string to arm the weapon. The strongest crossbow required the soldier to lie on his back and place his feet through the handle, then pull on the string to arm the weapon. The lighter versions could be armed with two hands.

55. Top and side views of a bronze Chinese crossbow mechanism with a butt plate. Note the *Wang Shan* aiming device atop the trigger housing.

56. A hand-held, trigger-operated crossbow. Note the presence of the pistol grip and trigger guard to prevent accidental or premature firing of the weapon.

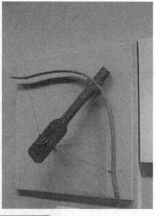

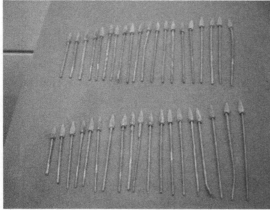

57. Crossbow and bolts, Shaanxi History Museum, Shaanxi, China.

The Han army had combined arms regiments with the crossbowmen as the primary fighting force and the infantry in support, not unlike modern artillery units with infantry security elements. The commander of such a unit was aptly called "The Crossbow General."

* * *

In time, the demand for more effective firepower brought about the development of the first rapid-fire weapon system in the world. Some unidentified entrepreneurial individual modified the crossbow by mounting a magazine box atop the bolt receiver groove. With ten bronze bolts in the magazine, the final product — the Lian Huan Nu (The Repeating Crossbow), became a rapid-fire weapon that shot ten bolts in less than fifteen seconds.

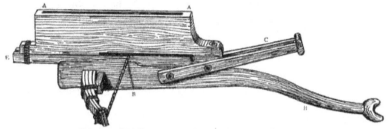

FIG. 171.—SIDE VIEW OF THE CHINESE REPEATING CROSSBOW.

58. Illustration from "The Crossbow", Ralph Payne-Gallwey, 1903 Longman's, Green & Co. London.

Archaeological evidence of the earliest repeating crossbow from Tomb 47 at Qin Jia Zui, Hubei Province, China has been dated to the Warring States Era, circa 400 BC. The modified weapon consisted of a long-U shaped lever, hinged by metal pins to the stock of the crossbow and the magazine. To arm and fire the repeating crossbow, a soldier simply held the stock firmly against his waist with one hand while he pushed the lever forward with the other. The lever action lifted the magazine box up and forward, then caught the bow string with a notch located at the rear bottom of the magazine. When the lever was pulled back, it returned the magazine to its original position atop the stock and at the same time drew the bow string to the ready-fire position. The bow string, while being pulled back, kept the reserve bolts in the magazine from dropping down prematurely. Once the lever was all the way back, the bowstring became clear of the bottom of the magazine well, thus allowing a bolt to drop into the firing groove atop the stock. As the magazine seated itself into its original position, a small firing toggle mounted at the bottom of the magazine was pushed up by the stock. The firing mechanism (toggle) sat in a notched hole at the base of the magazine box, with the small end protruding below the magazine box. The upside down conical shape of the trigger prevented it from falling through the notched hole during operation of the weapon. With the magazine box seated on the stock, the toggle was pushed upward and lifted the bow string out of its retaining notch to launch the bolt out of the crossbow. The procedure was repeated until the bolts in the magazine were exhausted.

It should be noted that the magazine was basically an open top box, so it could be reloaded with ease. The safe position of the weapon was just after a bolt had been shot out of the groove. Of course, accuracy was sacrificed for speed and volume of fire; however, a block of 10,000 men armed with the repeating crossbows could afford the luxury of a slight reduction in precision. Besides, poisoned tips added to the lethality of the bronze bolts.

The need to work the arming lever required another modification to the original crossbow. The butt of the weapon was extended, with a widened end to the stock to be pressed securely against the firer's waist during operations; this enhanced leverage and stability during firing of the weapon. Consequently, the repeating crossbow was usually fired from the waist with the repeating crossbowman in the standing position, rather than the aimed shoulder firing method of the traditional crossbow.

The standard effective range of the repeating crossbow was about seventy-five paces, with the maximum firing range of two hundred paces. A further modified version of the weapon consisted of twin magazines and two shooting grooves in the center of the framework, which doubled the firepower.

As for its use in combat, like the modern artillery, it was an ideal weapon for firing opening salvos at a massed enemy formation either in the attack or defense during open field combat. It was also an excellent weapon for ambushes and for fighting massed charges by lightly armored nomadic cavalry. Supported by armored infantrymen, the massed volleys of missiles from the repeating crossbowmen could blunt nomadic charges.

Military formations of the Imperial Ch'in Dynasty (221 to 206 BC) deployed crossbowmen in front of its infantry. Theoretically, the crossbowmen withdrew behind the infantry when the enemy approached for close combat. The Imperial Tang Dynasty (AD 618 to 907) military doctrine dictated firing the crossbows when the enemy closed to one hundred and fifty paces and the recurve bows at sixty paces, and resorting to the Mo Dao (Long Sword) within twenty paces for close combat.

The crossbowmen were also deployed to provide rear and flank security for the army on the move. In the fixed defensive mode, repeating crossbows were often mounted on firing platforms to provide extra stability and increased accuracy for the weapon. Repeating crossbows were also mounted on Chinese warships as an anti-personnel weapon. Historians have recorded that the First Emperor of China, Ch'in Shi Huang Di, used a crossbow(s) to kill a sea monster which had been threatening the maritime expedition that he had dispatched to search for the elixir of eternal life. The record did not specify the type of crossbow used on that occasion. It might have been a larger version like a Roman scorpion, which fired a harpoon-like bolt.

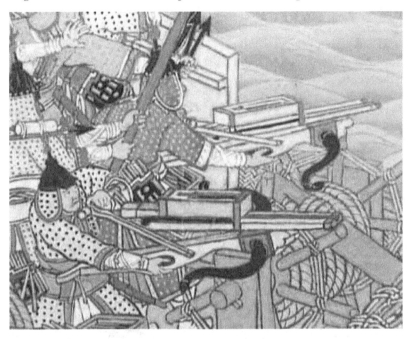

59. Ship mounted Repeating Crossbow. Note the widened stock pressed against the soldier's waist.

* * *

At the Battle of Ma-Ling (341 BC), Sun Bin, a descendent of Sun Tzu (the author of *The Art of War*), led a 30,000-man Qi army and defeated his opponent Pan Juan, who commanded the 100,000-man Wei army. The crucial encounter came in a night ambush by 10,000 crossbowmen against Pan Juan's vanguard of 10,000 men. Pang Juan, who had previously framed and crippled Sun Bin, committed suicide by cutting his own throat. Historic texts do not specify the type(s) of crossbows used in that ambush. It was probably a combination of the standard and repeating versions.

* * *

Kong Ming, an innovator and strategist of the late Han Dynasty, modified the original crossbow by designing a giant platform, then mounting multiple oversized crossbows onto a single frame with a trigger mechanism to fire them at the same time. It was something like the Roman ballista, except Kong Ming's version fired ten bolts at the same time. His giant crossbow became known as *Zhuge Nu* or *Zhuge Lian Nu*, which literally translates into 'Kong Ming's Crossbow' or 'Kong Ming's Linked Bow.'

The name of *Zhuge Nu* or *Zhuge Lian Nu* was sometimes misapplied to the repeating crossbow (*Lian Huan Nu*). The Zhuge Nu was a crew-served weapon that required seven or eight men to load and fire. By contrast the repeating crossbow could be operated by one soldier alone, and although it could fire ten bolts rapidly, it fired the bolts one at a time. In addition, Kong Ming lived during the Han Dynasty, at least 500 years after the appearance of the repeating crossbow during the Spring and Autumn Era.

* * *

Due to the time-consuming reloading requirement, crossbowmen armed with standard crossbows usually required protection and support from infantry or longbow archers. Crossbow regiments were often organized into 'arming,' 'loading,' and 'firing' elements to ensure a continuous rain of missiles toward the enemy; not unlike the Western European musket regiments of the 18th and 19th centuries. The crossbow fell into decline due in part to the increased dominance of the cavalry and the slow loading process of the weapon. Its cumbersomeness plus the economic and logistical cost of manufacturing metal bolts gradually relegated it primarily to the defensive role. The advent of gunpowder weapons sounded the death knell for the crossbow.

* * *

60. Repeating Crossbow of the Imperial Qing Dynasty (AD 1644–1911). Note the lack of aiming device and trigger mechanism standard with a normal crossbow.

In more recent times, during the Sino-Japanese War (1894–1895), some of the stunningly ill-equipped Imperial Qing soldiers went into battle armed with the repeating crossbows designed by their ancestors 2,500 years ago. The ancient weapon was last known to be used by Chinese warriors of the Justice and Peace Society during the Boxer Rebellion (1898–1901) against the armies of eight allied foreign powers that invaded China: the Japanese, Russian, British, German, and Austro-Hungarian Empires, the French Third Republic, the United States, and the Kingdom of Italy.

* * *

Final note — a miniature version of the repeating crossbow was found in the pillow box of an ancient Chinese tomb. It might have been an olden-days counterpart of the modern day derringer, used for personal security.

BIBLIOGRAPHY

Sun Tzu, *The Art of War*. Translated and with an introduction by Samuel B. Griffith. Oxford University Press. London, 1963.

Sun Tzu's The Art of War. Chinese–English, translated by Lo Zhiye. Taiwan Commercial Shop, Ltd. Taipei, 1995.

The Crossbow, Ralph Payne-Gallwey, Longman's, Green & Co. London, 1903.

Valiant Imperial Warriors 2200 Years Ago – Terra-cotta Armoured Warriors and Horses of Qin Shi Huang Mausoleum. Wu Xiaocong. Polyspring Company Ltd. Hong Kong, 1992.

Bai Hua Shi Ji 白话史记。 'Literary Translation of Historical Chronicles.' (3 volumes) Edited by Literary Translation of Historical Chronicles Committee. United Management Publishing Industry Corporation. Taipei, 1985.

Dong Zhou Lie Guo Zhi 东周列国志。 'Chronicles of the Eastern Zhou Kingdoms.' Feng Menglong. Sanming Book Publishing, Ltd. Taipei, 1976.

Dong Zhou Lie Guo Zhi 东周列国志。 'Chronicle of the Eastern Zhou Kingdom.' (2 Volumes.) Original work of Feng Menglong, revised by Cai Yuanfang. Sanming Book Publishing, Ltd. Taipei, 2008.

Dong Zhou Lie Guo Zhi 东周列国志。 'Chronicle of the Eastern Zhou Kingdom.' Original work of Feng Menglong, revised by Liu Peirong. Mingtien Cultural, Ltd. Taipei, 2004.

Qin Han Shi 秦汉史。 'History of Qin and Han Dynasties.' Jian Bozhan, Yuenlong Publishing. Taipei, 2003.

Qin Han Shi Hua 秦汉史话。 'Historical Commentaries of Qin and Han Dynasties.' Chen Zhiping. Sanming Book Publishing, Ltd. Taipei, 2008.

Sun Wu Bing Fa 孙吴兵法。 'Sun and Wu Military Treatises.' Ministry of Defense, General Political Warfare Department. Taiwan, 1978.

Zhàn Guó Shi Dài 戰國時代。'Warring States Era.' Bo Yang. United Management Publishing Industry Corporation. Taipei, 1984.

Wu Jing Zong Yao 武经总要。 *Military Encyclopedia or Complete Essentials for the Military Classics, Song Dynasty, 1044 AD.*

Wu Qi Bing Fa 吴起兵法。 'Wu Qi's Military Treatise.' Edited by Li Tiandao. Chinese Language Web, Ltd. Taipei, 2003.

*Xian Qin Zu Zhi Bai Jia Zheng Ming*先秦诸子百家争鸣。 'Hundred Schools of Thoughts During Early Qin Era.' Yi Zhongtian. Tai Dian Electronics Industry. Taipei, Taiwan, 2009.

*Zhan Lue Zhan Shu Bing Qi Shi Dian (1) Zhong Guo Gu Dai Pian*战略战术兵器事典 (1) 中国古代篇。 'Compendium of Strategy Tactics and Weapons Volume 1 – Ancient China Edition. Translated by Zhang Yongxiang, Gakken Publishing Company, Ltd. Tokyo, 2011.

Zhong Guo Jiang Shuai Shi Lue 中国将帅事略。 'Assorted Deeds of Chinese Generals.' Zhang Yunfeng. Great Earth Publishing, Taipei, 2007.

Zhong Guo Jiang Yu De Bian Qian 中国疆域的变迁。 'Transformations of China's borders.' (2 volumes.) Li Tianming. National Palace Museum, Taipei, Taiwan. 1997.

Zhong Guo Shi Xueh Shi 中国史学史。 'Historical Study of Chinese History.' (2 volumes.) Du Weiyuen. Sanming Book Publishing, Ltd. Taipei, 1998.

Zhong Guo Tong Shi 中国通史。 'General History of China.' (2 volumes.) Lo Xianglin. Zhengzhong Publishing. Taipei, 1977.

Zhong Guo Zher Xueh Jian Shi 中国哲学简史。 'An Abbreviated History of Chinese Philosophy.' Feng Youlan. New World Press. Beijing, 2004.

Zhong Hua Wu Qian Nian Shi Hua 中华五千年史话。 'History of 5000 years of China.' Guo Bonan and Liu Fuyuan. Joint Publishing (H.K.) Co., Ltd. Hong Kong, 1988.

*Zī Zhì Tōng Jiàn*资治通鉴。 'Comprehensive Mirror A Record of Chinese History.' (2 volumes) Shima Guang. Beijing, 2003.

A

An-Ee, capital of the Wei kingdom, 75
An-Yang, 92
Attack Wei to Rescue Zhao, 84
Attila the Hun, 7, 32

B

Bai Chi (AKA: Duke Wu An (d. 257 BC) –
The most successful general in Chinese
history, the Alexander the Great of
China. Famous for maneuver warfare,
and the defeat of numerically superior
foes, 7, 21, 47, 48, 50-52, 54-56, 58-63,
65, 87, 93, 141
Bai Chi Canal, 52
Bao Yuan – General of the Han kingdom
at the led the Han force at the Battle of
Yi Jue (293 BC), 50, 51
Bare Head Brigade, 6, 22, 58, 103-107
Battle of Bo-Ju, 121
Battle of Cannae, 98
Battle of Chang-Ban, 118
Battle of Chang-Ping (260 BC), 21, 52-55,
59-62, 87, 140, 141
Battle of Gai Xia, 98
Battle of Guei Ling, 82, 83
Battle of Jin-Yang, 131-133
Battle of the Red Cliff, 68, 117, 120
Battles of Yan and Ying (279 BC), 51
Battle of Yi Jue (293 BC), 48

Battle of Zui-Li, 125-127
Bed Crossbow, 13, 14
Bodkin arrowheads, 21
Bo-Ju, 121-123, 126
Bo Pi – A courtier of the Wu state, War-
ring States Era, 127-130
Boxer Rebellion (1898–1901), 32, 170
Boxer Rebellion Indemnity Scholarship,
32

C

Cai kingdom, 121
Cao Cao – Chancellor of the Han Empire
and leader of the Wei kingdom, 68, 71,
118-120
Chang-An, 163
Chang-Ping, 21, 52-55, 59-62, 87, 140, 141
Chang Ynew – A general of the Qi king-
dom, 74, 75
Cheng (乘) – A chariot company consist-
ing of one war chariot and 75 men, 5,
52-54, 69, 70, 85, 122
Cheng, capital of the Chu kingdom, 31, 51,
52, 122
Chiang Kai-Shek – Leader of the Kuo-
mingtang, Nationalist Party, Republic
of China (Taiwan), 24-26
Ch'in (Qin) Dynasty, 30, 91, 93, 96, 97, 168
Chinese Crossbow, 165, 166
Chu kingdom, 31, 36, 51, 52, 62, 71, 78, 80,
93, 96, 110, 121-123, 125, 129
Ch'in Wu-Yang – An assassin recruited

by Crown Prince Dan, 153, 154, 156

Chu Wu – Courtier of the Yan State and teacher of Crown Prince Dan, 141

Cloud Ladder, 15

Confucius – Famous Chinese scholar, philosopher, teacher, accomplished musician, administrator and military leader, 31, 36, 37, 72

Cook, General – US army general who pursued Chief Geronimo in the southwestern US Indian Territory, 68

Crossbow, 13, 14, 68, 106, 165-171, 173

Crown Prince Dan – Crown Prince of the Yan kingdom. The instigator of the attempted assassination of King Zheng, 65, 139-148, 150-154, 156, 157

Crown Prince Si – Heir of Duke Xiao of the Ch'in kingdom, 43, 157

D

Da-Liang, the Capital of the Wei kingdom, 43, 82-84

Dan Gong (弹弓) – Sling shot, 165

Dee Heng – A courtier in the Wei Royal Court and sponsor of Wu Qi to Lord Wen, 75

Deng Xiao-Ping – President and Chairman of the People's Republic of China, 26

Dagger Ax or Ge, 19

Diminishing Hearth Fires, 84, 89

Ding-Tao, 92

Dong-Yang, early Capital of the Ch'in kingdom, 40, 42

Door Jammer, 17

Double agents, 24

Dowager Empress Zheng – Ruler of the Han Empire, 89

Death Warrior, 139

Du Keng, 146, 148, 152

Duke Hui – The ruler of the Ch'in kingdom, 75

Duke Jing – Ruler of the Qi state, 36, 37

Duke Mu – The ruler of the Lu state, 73-75

Duke of Ma Fu, 87

Duke Ping Yuan – A prominent courtier, and brother of King Hui Wen, 85

Duke Wen – Ruler of the Lu state, 36, 37

Duke Xiao – Ruler of the Ch'in State who hired San Yang, 40, 43

Du Yew, 61

E

Elite Warrior Corps (Wu Ju Zhi), 75, 76, 104

Emperor Han Wu (157 – 87 BC) – The Seventh Emperor of the Han Dynasty, 6

Empty City Strategy, 68, 69

Equine ships, 136

Eunuchs, 135, 154, 155, 157

F

Fang-Cheng, 122

Fan Sui – The Prime Minister of the Ch'in kingdom., 54, 59, 61, 65

Fan-Wu, 86

Fan Yu-Chi – Renegade general of the Ch'in kingdom. He donated his head in the assassination effort against King Zheng, 147

Fei Go (see Flying Hook)

Feng Ting – General and the Han commander at the Battle of Chang-Ping, 53, 56-58

Fire Dragon, 17, 18

Flame Thrower, 19

Flying Hook, 16

Fu Bao – General of the Zhao army at the Battle of Chang-Ping, 56

Fuchuan warships, 136

Fu Gai – Younger brother of King He Lu of the Wu kingdom, 122

G

Gan Luo – Young diplomatic genius of the Ch'in kingdom, 65, 66

Gan Mao – Grandfather of Gan Luo, 65

Ge (弓), See Dagger Ax

Geronimo – The Apache Indian chief who was pursued by General Cook in the US southwest territory, 68

Ghu City, 72, 111-113

Gon Ei Hsiu – The prime minister of Lu

kingdom and sponsor of Wu Qi, 73

Gong Su – A prime minister of the Wei kingdom, 78

Gong-Sun Jia – The teacher of Crown Prince Xi, 43

Gong-Sun Xi – General of the Wei kingdom and the nominal Commander-in-Chief of the Han-Wei alliance at the Battle of Yi Jue (293 BC), 50, 51

Gong-Tse Ang – The Crown Prince and Commander of the Wei army who was kidnapped and defeated by San Yang, 43

Gong-Tse Qian – The royal advisor to Crown Prince Si, 43

Green Society Triad, 25

Guan Ying – Han cavalry general famous for chasing down Xiang Yu with a force of 5000 cavalrymen, 6

Guan Yu (AKA: Guan Gong) – War god of China. Famous for his loyalty, sense of honor, and his martial feats. Guan Dao, the two-meter-long knife, was named after him, 7, 37, 38, 120

Gui Gu Zi – A mythical sage who had trained many famous leaders of the Warring States Era, 81

Gui-Ji, 127

Gu-Li, 111

Gu-Xu, 128, 129

Guy Nieh – Master swordsman of the Zhao kingdom, able to kill a bird in flight with his sword, 148, 150, 151, 154, 157

H

Han-Dan, 55, 59-61, 65, 82, 83, 86, 92, 148, 149

Han Dynasty (206 BC–AD 220), 3, 6, 32, 71, 100, 158, 160, 165, 169, 170

Han-Gu-Guan fortress, 48, 51

Han kingdoms, 48, 140

Han Hu – Senior Minister of the Jin court, founder of the Han kingdom, 131, 132

Han River, 51, 122, 123

Han Xin – A rebel leader of the late Ch'in Dynasty, 98

He-Jian territories, 66

Hong Gou River, 97

Hong-Meng, 97

Horse Slayer Knife (AKA: The Three Heads Knife), 160

Hsia Fu – An assassin recruited by Crown Prince Dan, 142, 147

Huai River, 111, 121, 122

Huang Pu Military Academy, 26

Hua-Rong Pass, 120

Hu Ben (Leaping Tigers) – Chinese elite troops., 6

Hufuhuqi 胡服胡骑 – Nomadic Outfits and Nomadic Riders, 6

Hu Yang – A Ch'in general, 85-87

Huang Guy – Naval commander of Sun Quan's navy, 119

J

Jade Emperor of Heaven, 113

Japan, 25, 32, 135, 163

Japanese Samurai sword, 159, 163

Jet Propulsion Laboratory, Caltech, 24

Ji (戟), a Ge with a spearhead attached to the top., 20

Ji, Capital of the Yan kingdom, 20, 25, 26, 35, 66, 82, 83, 98, 99, 110, 144, 173

Jiagu Mountain, 36

Jiān Jūn 监军 – Adjutant General, 7

Jiang-Ling, 118

Jianwen – The second emperor of the Ming dynasty. He was overthrown in 1403 by Yong Li, 135, 137

Jih-Moh, 109, 112-116

Jin kingdom, 5, 45, 131, 133

Jing Jian – Ch'in courtier who recommended San Yang to Duke Xiao, 40

Jing Ke – The most famous assassin of Chinese history, 139, 142-158

Jing-Zhou, 118, 120

Jin-Yang, 131-133

Ju Li – A son of Ju Yuan-Zhang, the founder and the First Emperor of the Imperial Ming Dynasty. Ju Li staged a successful coup d'état against his nephew and became Emperor Yong Li., 135

Ju-Lu, 92, 93, 96

Jun （军）– A unit of 12,500 men. In modern military terms, it is an army., 4, 5, 34, 37, 104

Jun Zi (君子) Knight, 34

K

Ke Tou Jun, see Bare Head Brigade

King Diao – Ruler of the Chu kingdom, 78-80

King Gou Jian – son of King Yun and the ruler of the Yue kingdom., 127

King He Lu – King of the Wu kingdom, Warring States Era, 36, 121-123, 125-128

King Huai – King of Chu kingdom of late Ch'in Dynasty, 92, 96

King Hui – Ruler of the Wei nation who refused to hire San Yang, 40, 43

King Hui – King of the Yan nation, 110, 114

King Hui Wen – Ruler of the Zhao kingdom, 51, 85

King Min – Son of Shuan and King of Qi state, 110-113

King Ping – King of the Chu kingdom. He murdered Wu Tzu She's father and brother, 31

King Shuan – King of Qi state, 110

King Si – Father of Crown Prince Dan and King of the Yan state, 157

King Tso – Son of Hui and King of the Yan state, 110, 113

King Wuling – King of the Zhao kingdom and creator of the Chinese cavalry in 307 BC, 5, 6

King Xiao Cheng – King of Zhao kingdom at the Battle of Chang-Ping, 53, 54

King You Miao – Ruler of the Zhao kingdom, 65, 66

King Yun – King of the Yue nation, 125

King Zhao Xiang – Ruler of the Ch'in kingdom, 49-51, 58, 60-63

King Zhao – King of the Chu kingdom, 54, 59, 65, 66, 82, 122, 132, 148, 149

Kong-Chang Ridge, 53

Kong Ming (AKA: Zhu-Ge Liang, 181– AD 234) – Accomplished scholar, statesman, military strategist, administrator, inventor, astrologer, and meteorologist. The Chinese Leonardo DaVinci, 67-70, 169, 170

Korean War, 9, 25, 26

Kuomintang, 24, 26

L

Lament at Gai-Xia, 99

Lang Ya Pai (see Wolf Fang Smasher)

Lao Tzu – The founder of Daoism, 31

Leh Cheng – A general of the Zhao kingdom, 85

Leh Yi – General of the Yan army, 110-114

Lian （连）– A company, 5

Lian Huan Nu (See Repeating Crossbow)

Lian Poh – General of the Zhao kingdom at the Battle of Chang-Ping, 53-55, 59, 60, 85

Liang (两) – A unit of 25 men., 4

Liang Shima – Commander of a Liang., 4

Lin Biao – Graduate of Huang Pu Military Academy, Marshal of the People's Liberation Army, People's Republic of China, 26

Lin Tse, the Capital of the Qi nation, 74, 110, 112

Liu Bang – Founder and First Emperor of the Han Dynasty, 32, 95-98, 100

Liu Bei – Warlord of the Three Kingdom Era, 7, 31, 68, 70, 118, 120

Liu Biao – Warlord of late Han dynasty and ruler of Jing-Zhou, 118

Liu Cong – Son of Liu Biao, 118

Li Yi Zhi Bang (礼仪之邦), 31

Local informants, 24

Long Snake Arrow Box, 17, 18

Longbows, 21

Lord Wen – Ruler of the Wei kingdom, 75, 76

Lord Wu – A son of Lord Wen. He became ruler of the Wei kingdom after Lord Wen died, 76-78

Lu （旅）– A unit of 500 men. In modern military terms, it is a brigade., 4, 36

Lu Bu-Wei – Prime Minister of the Ch'in kingdom, 65

Lu kingdom, 37, 72-75

M

Ma-Ling, 82-84, 89, 169

Ma Su – A general under Kong Ming's command, 68

Mei Ren Ji 美人計 (Strategy of Beauties)

Meng Huo – Rebel leader who fought and

was caught then released seven times by Kong Ming, 68

Meng Jia – Ch'in courtier and unwitting accomplice to the assassination plot against King Zheng, 151, 152, 156, 157

Ming Dynasty (1368–1644), 135

Mo Dao, 159-161, 163, 168

Moltke, Helmut von ('No battle plan survives contact with the enemy.'), 90

N

Nang Wa – Prime Minister of the Chu kingdom, 122, 123

Nao Tsi – General of the Chu army, 111

Nest Cart, 14

Nie Rong Ji 聂荣臻 – Graduate of Huang Pu Military Academy, Marshall of the People's Liberation Army, People's Republic of China, 26

Nine Bronze Ceremonial Urns – the symbol of authority and power, 110

Nomads, 3, 5, 6, 32, 160, 168

North Korea, 32

P

Pai （排）– A modern Chinese army platoon., 5, 16

Pang Juan – A general in the Wei kingdom, 81-84, 169

Pang Tong – A defector from the Wu kingdom to Cao Cao at the Battle of Red Cliff, 118, 119

Patrol ships, 136

Penetration agents, 24

People's Liberation Army (PLA), 9, 26, 27

Pontoon Bridge, 15

Prince Dan – Crown Prince of the Yan nation who was an exchange hostage at Xian-Yang, 65, 139-148, 150-154, 156, 157

Prince Fa Tsang – Son of King Min and King of the Qi state, 111

Prince Jia – The Crown Prince of the Zhao state, 43, 144, 151, 152, 156, 157, 167, 174

Q

Qian Xuesen (钱学森, 11 December 1911 – 31 October 2009, 24

Qi Jie – A general of the Yan army. He replaced Leh Yi, 112-115

Qi kingdom, 72-74, 82, 83, 110, 111, 129, 140

Qingbang (See Green Society Triad)

Qin Gui, 31

Qing Dynasty (1644–1911), 170

R

Recruited assets, 24

Repeating crossbow, 106, 167-171

Rituals and Etiquette (Li Yi Zhi Bang), 31

Romance of the Three Kingdoms, 31, 70

S

San Yang (AKA: Way Yang, 395-338 BC) – The Iron Chancellor, Architect of Imperial Chinese bureaucracy, 39, 43, 44, 46, 47, 79, 80, 104

Shang-Dang territory, 53

Shang Dynasty (1523 – 1046 BC), 4-6, 19, 165

Shen Bao Xu – A Chu courtier who got the Ch'in state to evict the Wu invaders, 123

Shen Yin Shu – General of the Chu army, 122

Shi （師）– Ancient military unit of 2,500 men. In modern military terms, it is a division., 4, 5, 60, 129, 158, 163, 168, 173, 174

Shih-Ma Geng – Ch'in general at the Battle of Chang-Ping, 53, 55

Shih-Ma Tsou – General of the Ch'in army at the Battle of Chang-Ping, 55

Shi-Ma Yi – General of the Wei kingdom, 69, 70

Sino-Japanese War (1894–1895), 170

Short Ge, 20

Shun Wu – General of the Jin kingdom whose army abandoned the chariot in favor of the infantry. See Wei Shun., 5

Sino-Vietnamese War, 9, 27

Six Arts (Rituals, Music, Archery, Chari-otry, Books, Numbers), 33, 34, 36, 37

Smashed Stoves and Sunken Ships, 91, 93

Song Dynasty (960–1279), 12, 13, 30, 174

Song Yi (of the Chu kingdom) – Courtier and commander of King Huai's army, 92, 93

Song Yi (assassin) recruited by Crown Prince Dan, 142, 147

Spring and Autumn Era (770–476 BC), 1, 5, 21, 35, 36, 45, 104, 121, 123, 131, 133, 170

Standard Trebuchet, 11, 12

Strategy of Beauties, 25

Su Dai – Courtier and diplomat of Zhao kingdom who secured an armistice af-ter the Battle of Chang-Ping, 59, 60

Suicide spies, 24

Su kingdom, 68, 70

Sun Bin – A scion of Sun Tzu. Military strategist of the Qi kingdom, 81-84, 89, 169

Sun Quan – Warlord of late Han dynasty and ruler of the Wu kingdom, 118, 119

Sun Tzu – Famous Chinese military strat-egist, author of The Art of War, 1, 23, 24, 31, 36, 71, 74, 79, 81, 109, 121-123, 125-127, 129, 169, 173

Supply ships, 136

Suzhou, 136

T

Taiwan, 26, 29, 37, 38, 70, 173, 174

Tang Dynasty (AD 618 –907), 7, 160, 161, 163, 168

Tang state (of Warring States Era), 7, 65, 66, 121, 160, 161, 163, 168

Tai-Xing Mountains, 53

Thunder Fire Ball, 18

Tien Dan – A minor official of the Qi state and commander of Jih-Moh, 112-116, 153

Tien Ghu – Courtier and a minister of the Qi kingdom, 72

Tien He – Prime Minister of the Qi king-dom who usurped the throne, 73, 74

Tien Ji – General of the Qi kingdom, 82, 83

Tien Wen – Courtier and prime minister of the Wei kingdom, 77, 78

Tiger Seal – An 8cm-long bronze prowl-ing tiger statue with bright golden cal-ligraphy painted on the body, 8

Tired Horse Ridge, 54

Traction Trebuchet, 11, 12

Treasure ships, 136

Troop ships, 136

Tseng Sen – A learned scholar and son of Tseng Tsan, who was a renowned dis-ciple of Confucius, 72, 73

Tuan (团)– A regiment., 5

Tun Zhang – Leader of a five-man unit or Wu, 4

Tzu Ying – The last Emperor of the Ch'in dynasty, 97

W

Wang Ben – General of the Ch'in army at the Battle of Chang-Ping, 55

Wang He – General of the Ch'in army at the Battle of Chang-Ping, 53-56, 61

Wang Jian – A general of the Ch'in army, 59, 144, 148

Wang Li – A Ch'in general, 92, 93

Wang Ling – General of the Ch'in army at the Battle of Chang-Ping, 55, 60, 61

Wang Shan or Watch Mountain – Cross-bow aiming device, 165

Wang Zong – General of the Zhao army at the Battle of Chang-Ping, 56

War Lord King of Western Chu, 96

Warring States Era (475–221 BC), 1, 4, 5, 7, 11, 13, 21, 22, 36, 45, 48, 62, 72, 81, 87, 92, 96, 97, 104, 110, 133, 167, 174

Water tankers, 136

Way kingdom, 13, 27, 29, 39, 40, 51, 56, 57, 59, 65, 66, 72, 84, 93, 97, 99, 100, 104, 114, 118, 120, 142, 146, 149, 151, 154, 155, 167

Wei Ju – Senior Minister of the Jin court, founder of the Wei kingdom., 132

Wei kingdom, 39, 43, 44, 50, 68, 69, 71, 75, 76, 82, 83, 104, 140

Wei River, 43, 53-55, 59

Wei She – General of the Chu army, 122

Wen Zhong – Minister of the Yue state, 127

West River territories (land west of the Yellow River), 75-78

Witches' Thunder, 16

Wolf Fang Smasher, 16

Wu (伍) – A unit of five, the basic element of a military formation., 4-7, 12, 31, 36, 47, 48, 52, 56, 57, 59-61, 68, 71-80, 89, 93, 99, 100, 104, 119, 121-123, 125-132, 141, 157, 163, 173, 174

Wu-An, 86

Wu-Cheng (Wu city), 72, 75, 79

Wu Cheng Hei – General of the Chu army, 122

Wu Du, 89

Wu Jing Zong Yao, Military Encyclopedia AKA: Complete Essentials for the Military Classics, Song Dynasty, AD 1044., 12, 15, 16, 18, 19, 174

Wu kingdom, 31, 36, 68, 76, 121, 125, 127-129

Wu-Lin, 118, 119

Wu Qi – Famous general and compatriot of Sun Tzu. Comparable to Julius Caesar in accomplishments, he created the "Elite Soldiers" system. Wu fought over 70 major campaigns and never suffered a defeat, except in the court of intrigue, 6, 71-80, 104, 174

Wu River, 76, 93, 99, 100

Wu Tze She (also Wu Ze Xu) – General and Prime Minister of the Wu kingdom who accompanied Sun Tzu in defeating the Chu kingdom, 31, 27, 129, 130

X

Xia-Kou, 118

Xiao Shan, 89

Xi Cheng, 69, 70

Xi Shi – A beautiful woman sent by Gou Jian to Fu Chai as tribute, 129

Xian – An Emperor of the Han Dynasty, 26, 52, 117, 174

Xian-Yang – Capital of the Ch'in (Qin) kingdom and later the Imperial Ch'in Empire., 3, 42-44, 54, 58-61, 63, 65, 66, 93, 96, 97, 139-141, 144, 145, 148, 150-152

Xiang Liang – A rebel commander of the late Imperial Ch'in Empire, 92

Xiang Yu – Powerful warlord of latter Ch'in dynasty, famous for his "Strategy of Smashed Stoves and Sunken Ships." However, he fell for the "Victory Chorus" ruse in 202 BC which cost him his kingdom and his life., 6, 91-93, 95-100

Xiao Bie Mountains, 122

Xia Wu-Chi – Royal physician of the Ch'in court who flung his medical box at Jing Keh to save the king's life, 155

Xiongnu – Nomads, 3, 5-7

Xu, 26, 89, 90, 121, 123, 127, 129, 130

Xu Xian Qian – Graduate of Huang Pu Military Academy, Marshall of the People's Liberation Army, People's Republic of China, 26

Y

Yang-Di, the Capital of Han kingdom, 83

Yanjing (modern day Beijing), 135

Yan kingdom, 65, 66, 110, 111, 139, 140, 149, 152, 156, 157

Yangtze River, 98, 118-120

Yang You-Ji, 21

Yeh Cha Lei (See Witches' Thunder)

Yeh-Wang city, 53

Ye Jian Ying 叶剑英 – Graduate of Huang Pu Military Academy, Marshall of the People's Liberation Army, People's Republic of China, 26

Yi Jue mountain pass, 50

Ying (营)– A battalion, 5, 6, 26, 31, 51, 52, 61, 97, 122, 123

Yi River, 50, 139, 148, 151, 157

Yi Yi Dai Lao (Wait and rest, then fight the tired ones), 25

Yue kingdom, 125, 127-129, 131

Yueh Fei, 31

Yu Ji – Favorite concubine of Xiang Yu, 98, 99

Yu Xi river valley, 53

Yu Xu – Han general and strategist, 89, 90

Yu-Yu, 85-87

Z

Zhang Fei– Sworn brother of Liu Bei, 31

Zhang Han – A Ch'in general., 92, 93

Zhang Tang – Courtier and general of the Ch'in kingdom, 65, 66

Zhan Ma Dao (See Horse Slayer Knife

Zhao Chieh – Zhao general at the Battle of Chang-Ping, 53

Zhao Gao – A minor eunuch of the Ch'in court who saved King Zheng's life by helping him draw his sword., 155, 157

Zhao Gua – General of the Zhao army at the Battle of Chang-Ping, 54-59, 87, 141

Zhao kingdom, 5, 6, 51, 53, 54, 59-62, 65, 82, 85, 86, 113, 148, 150

Zhao Liang – A friend of San Yang who warned San Yang about the consequence of court intrigue, 43

Zhao Ser – The Duke Ma Fu and father of Zhao Gua, 54, 85-87

Zhao Wu Min – Senior Minister of the Jin court and head of the Zhao clan, 132

Zheng (AKA: Ch'in Shih Huang Di) – The First Emperor of China. The great grandson of King Zhao Xiang, 13

Zheng Dan – A beautiful woman sent by Gou Jian to Fu Chai as tribute, 129

Zheng He, Admiral (AKA: Ma He, 4, 135-137, 149

Zhi Yao – Senior Minister of the Jin court, 131, 132

Zhong Wu, 121

Zhou Dynasty, 1, 5, 34

Zhuge Nu or Zhuge Lian Nu – manually loaded ten-bolt crossbow, 170

Zu (卒) – A soldier, 4, 174

Zu leader – Commander of a Zu, 4